MW01077574

STREAMLINERS

LOCOMOTIVES AND TRAINS IN THE AGE OF SPEED AND STYLE

BRIAN SOLOMON

Voyageur
Press

To the memory of my grandfather, Alfred P. Solomon, who experienced many of the great streamlined trains.

Quarto is the authority on a wide range of topics.

Quarto educates, entertains and enriches the lives of our readers—enthusiasts and lovers of hands-on living.

www.quartoknows.com

First published in 2015 by Voyageur Press, an imprint of Quarto Publishing Group USA Inc., 400 First Avenue North, Suite 400, Minneapolis, MN 55401 USA.
Telephone: (612) 344-8100 Fax: (612) 344-8692

© 2015 Quarto Publishing Group USA Inc.

All photographs are from the author's collection unless noted otherwise.

quartoknows.com
Visit our blogs at quartoknows.com

All rights reserved. With the exception of quoting brief passages for the purposes of review, no part of this publication may be reproduced without prior written permission from the Publisher.

The information in this book is true and complete to the best of our knowledge. All recommendations are made without any guarantee on the part of the author or Publisher, who also disclaims any liability incurred in connection with the use of this data or specific details.

We recognize, further, that some words, model names, and designations mentioned herein are the property of the trademark holder. We use them for identification purposes only. This is not an official publication.

Voyageur Press titles are also available at discounts in bulk quantity for industrial or sales-promotional use. For details write to Special Sales Manager at Quarto Publishing Group USA Inc., 400 First Avenue North, Suite 400, Minneapolis, MN 55401 USA.

To find out more about our books,
visit us online at www.voyageurpress.com.

ISBN: 978-0-7603-4747-8

Library of Congress Cataloging-in-Publication Data

Solomon, Brian, 1966- author.
 Streamliners : locomotives and trains in the age of speed and style / by Brian Solomon.
    pages cm
 Includes bibliography and index.
  ISBN 978-0-7603-4747-8 (hc)
 1. High speed trains--United States--History. 2. Express trains--United States--History. 3. Locomotives--United States--History. 4. Railroad passenger cars--United States--History. I. Title.
 TF573.S655 2015
 625.2'3--dc23
                    2015011948

Acquisitions Editors: Dennis Pernu and Steve Casper
Project Manager: Caitlin Fultz
Art Director: Cindy Samargia Laun
Cover Design: John Barnett
Book Design: Ryan Scheife
Layout: Rebecca Pagel

On the front cover: John E. Pickett

On the back cover: Brian Solomon

On the frontis: Southern Pacific's order for nine Electro-Motive E9A diesels in 1954 was its final streamlined passenger diesels. After retirement, SP 6051 was preserved and restored in the colorful *Daylight* paint scheme by California State Railroad Museum in Sacramento. *Brian Solomon*

On the title page: Delivered in 1935, Milwaukee Road's A1 Atlantics were the first American streamlined steam locomotives built new. Milwaukee bought four of them. In this view No. 2 departs Chicago with the *Hiawatha* for its 410-mile run via Milwaukee to the Twin Cities. They were capable of sustained high-speed running and routinely cruised at 100-plus miles per hour. *Vernon Seaver, Jay Williams collection*

On the contents page: One of Burlington's early *Zephyr*s was photographed at Keokuk, Iowa, on June 12, 1940. *Paul Stringham, Jay Williams collection*

Printed in China

10 9 8 7 6 5 4 3 2

CONTENTS

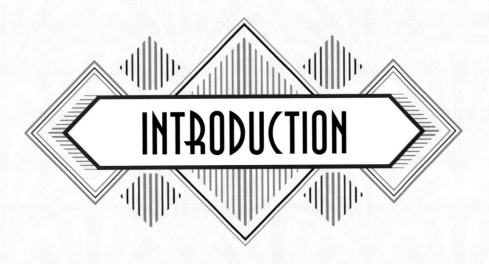

INTRODUCTION

The streamlined era represented the last phase of classic American railway travel and was the final effort by private railroads to improve their trains and keep the public moving by rail. What began as an effort to improve efficiency through aerodynamic design and adaptation of new systems of internal combustion propulsion rapidly evolved into whole new styles of train design. As the streamliner was transformed from the experimental showcase trains into more practical service vehicles, style and practicality took precedence over idealistic performance goals.

New styles and new technologies for trains were driven by developments in the rapidly evolving automobile, naval, and aircraft industries. By the mid-1930s, the combination of improved materials and new manufacturing techniques made possible radical changes to railway vehicle design. It was hoped that styling trains to be more like airplanes and automobiles would make them more popular. Railway equipment manufacturers had expectations that restyled trains would encourage railroads to buy new rolling stock during the height of the Great Depression when sales had hit an all-time low. In the short term it worked. However, the ultimate result of streamlining was different than originally anticipated.

During the 1930s, industrial designers swept into the scene and changed the way machines looked. Transport was at the forefront of this new movement, and railway trains were among their favorite machines to restyle. Visionaries such as Norman Bel Geddes, whose books were *Horizons* (1932) and *Magic Motorways* (1940), influenced a generation of transport design.

The decade that simultaneously saw the rise of lightweight railway passenger cars and the diesel locomotive also produced a host of advanced steam locomotives, many of which were styled with futuristic streamlined shrouds. Early streamlined steam emerged in an earnest effort to reduce wind resistance for fast passenger locomotives, while most of the later efforts were purely stylistic works to make steam power appear modern. The results varied from the sublime to the absurd. Unlike diesel trains, where streamlined superstructures were often integral with the whole machine, on steam power streamlined shrouding was superfluous. Many streamlined steam

Opposite: A lone Canadian-built Wabash F7A works in freight service on August 1, 1957. Streamlining set the tone for locomotive design for more than two decades. During the early years of postwar dieselization, many North American railroads bought streamlined-style diesels for both freight and passenger service. *Jim Shaughnessy*

Overleaf: Pennsylvania GG1 electric 4879 races between New York and Philadelphia at Edison, New Jersey, in 1963. The classic lines of the GG1 have long made it one of the most recognizable streamlined locomotives. *Jim Shaughnessy*

Two modes of transport featuring classic General Motors styling meet at Browns Road in Grafton, Massachusetts, on October 12, 2014. Paused at the grade crossing for Grafton & Upton's local freight led by the railroad's F7A 1501 is a 1970 Buick Skylark convertible. G&U is one of several short line railroads that continue to use classic streamlined diesels. *Steve Carlson*

locomotives eventually saw shrouds removed in whole or in part because the exterior coverings hampered maintenance. Among the most impressive styled steam designs were by Henry Dreyfuss for New York Central, Raymond Loewy for Pennsylvania Railroad, and Otto Kuhler for various lines.

By 1939 streamlined and lightweight forms had all but supplanted older designs for new passenger cars. Streamlined styles were virtually synonymous with road diesels, and even new freight locomotives were streamlined. Sleek compound curves and smooth surfaces seemed to convey modernity and power, and they dominated the appearance of railway design for the next decade and a half.

Streamlining helped sell dieselization. Yet despite the diesel, railroads rapidly lost market share to their competition after World War II. By the mid-1950s, streamlining lost its favor with railroads. New locomotives took on a new generation of utilitarian shapes. The passenger train appeared to be in terminal decline, and efforts by manufacturers to develop a new generation of fast, streamlined lightweight trains to help save the floundering passenger business were largely ignored. Further efforts at introducing fast trains in the 1960s again saw a brief revival of streamlined

In 1930, Thomas Conway Jr. encouraged wind tunnel research to develop a new generation of lightweight, high-speed third-rail electric cars for his Philadelphia & Western suburban line. Built by Brill, P&W's ten "Bullet Cars" were among the earliest American railway vehicles to benefit directly from aerodynamic principles. On Christmas Day 1960, a P&W Bullet Car races from Norristown toward 69th street Upper Darby. *Richard Jay Solomon*

design, but by and large, railroading remained the domain of utilitarian shapes.

In more recent times, streamlined designs have continued to find favor for some passenger locomotives and trains. Overseas, high-speed train design continues to embrace a variety of modern aerodynamic forms, with many of the most impressive trains built by French, German, and Japanese manufacturers. In North America, modern efforts have assumed

sleek streamlined shapes, such as Electro-Motive's F59PHI passenger locomotive that debuted in the mid-1990s, and Amtrak's high-speed train, based in part on French TGV technology, designed in the late 1990s for *Acela Express* services. And the continued interest in classic streamliners has resulted in the revival and restoration of vintage equipment.

In this book, I've focused on several aspects of streamlined trains in North America, beginning with early interest in aerodynamics and the relationships between wind-resistant design, lightweight construction, and internal combustion propulsion. I highlight Pullman and Budd's original streamliners, which made widely followed public debuts in 1934 that stirred significant changes in American railroading. Most subsequent streamliners were developed either in emulation or reaction to those trains.

I've covered a great variety of the trains and locomotives developed between the mid-1930s and the mid-1950s and emphasized the influential roles of General Motors, Budd, Pullman, and other manufacturers, and I've detailed the individual work of industrial designers and engineers. Even though I've illustrated and discussed many of the most prominent streamlining efforts and covered some of the lesser-known or obscure streamlined trains, I've not attempted to make this a comprehensive work. There were a great many more streamliners working North American rails, especially in the postwar period, than space allows for full coverage in this modest book. I opted to concentrate and illustrate the classic period rather than the more recent developments. Modern high-speed trains are a topic for a future work.

S. R. CALTHROP.
Railway Car.

No. 49,227.

Patented Aug. 8, 1865.

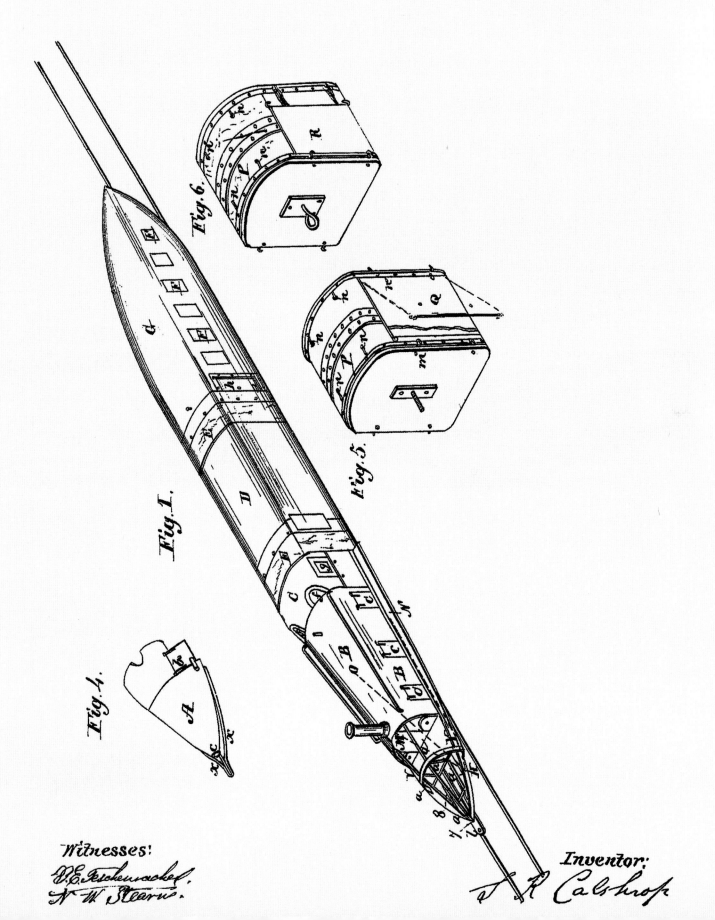

Fig. 6.

Fig. 5.

Fig. 1.

Fig. 4.

Witnesses:

Inventor:

S. R. Calthrop

CHAPTER 1

EXPERIMENTS, AERODYNAMICS, AND McKEEN MOTOR CARS

Early Investigations and Experiments in Wind Resistance

It had been long understood that smooth surfaces and natural forms reduced the resistance of bodies passing through water. In the late eighteenth and early nineteenth centuries, inquisitive minds transferred this concept to air resistance. In 1804, Sir George Cayley investigated air-resistant shapes, using sea animals as prototypes for his aeronautical designs. He proposed application of "oblong spheroid" designs for use as dirigibles (air ships). In a 1974 article in the academic journal *Leonardo*, "Streamlining and American Industrial Design," Donald J. Bush credits Cayley for recognizing by 1810 "the necessity of tapering the rear of the streamlined form to avoid a drop in air pressure that would increase drag."

The development of railways from the 1820s onward gradually resulted in larger and faster trains. The need to improve fuel economy occasionally revived interest in wind resistance, although nineteenth century efforts were fruitless. Among the earliest to experiment with wind resistance was British inventor Henry Bessemer. In *The American Passenger Car*, historian John H. White Jr. indicates that during the 1840s

Opposite & right: In 1865, American inventor Samuel R. Calthrop patented a wind-resistant train. His concept was generations ahead of his time, and his patent anticipated future developments. *United States Patent, 49,227, Aug. 8, 1865*

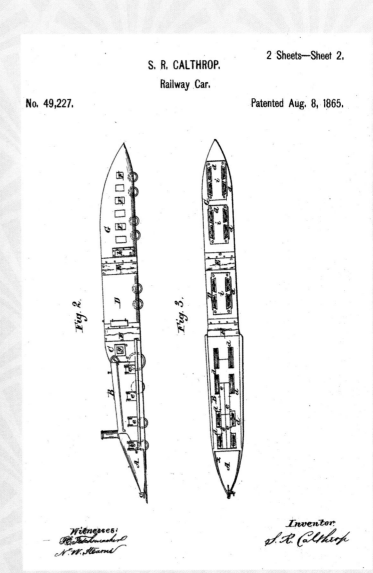

Bessemer conducted wind-resistant tests on railway passenger cars in the UK. His results do not appear to have influenced railway car design, but a decade later, Bessemer went on to refine a steel-making process for which he became world famous.

Another wind-resistance pioneer was American Samuel R. Calthrop, who in 1865 was awarded a patent for an "air-resisting" train. According to a biographical story written posthumously in the 1930s by his daughter, Edith Calthrop Bump, Calthrop's inspiration came from his experience walking railway lines and studying wear patterns along the rails in relation to places where high wind affected operations, and from discussions with railway men regarding the effects of wind on locomotive operation. In addition, he noted the effect of drafts between passenger cars when trains were at speed. Although lacking in a modern scientific approach, both his observations and his solutions were generations ahead of his time. In his patent, Caltrop wrote:

> The chief resistances opposed to the progress of a railway-train are those arising from the following causes: First, the friction of the machinery, which includes the friction of the wheels, their boxes [journal bearings], that of their surfaces bearing upon the rails, and the friction of the working parts of the engine itself; second, the pack-pressure on the piston of the steam which is forced through the blast-pipe; third, the resistance occasioned by the passage of the train through the atmosphere.

To address the problem of atmospheric resistance, Calthrop's ideas built upon those presented by Cayley and others earlier in the century. Specifically, he regarded "the whole train as an aerial ship" and looked to provide "its whole surface in accordance with the principles so successfully applied to ship-building." His patent proposed to shelter the mechanical portions of the train in an enclosure that was tapered at both front and rear ends (which he described in nautical terms as the "prow" and the rear as the "stern"). Furthermore, this design would use a "false bottom analogous to the case under the engine, under the tender, and under every car throughout their whole length . . . leaving only slits for their lower parts," while raising the top of the tender to a level equal with that of the following cars, and providing "a covered roof conforming its whole outline (top, bottom, and sides) to the general contour of the train, thus sheltering the

Opposite top: Frederick U. Adams' patent predated construction of his experimental train by seven years. Notice the similarities between Adams' train and that suggested by Calthrop decades earlier. *United States Patent, 189,911, Jan. 17, 1893*

Opposite bottom: Streamlining was a long time coming: Adams' patent from 1893 included flush doors and elaborate diaphragms between cars, ideas that were implemented forty years later on streamlined lightweight trains in the 1930s. *United States Patent, 189,911, Jan. 17, 1893*

first car from the direct resistance occasioned by the sudden depression of the tender." Significantly, his design minimized protrusions from a train's body, one of the keys to later streamlined trains, through the use of flush doors while covering spaces between locomotive, tender, and cars with flush, flexible "hoods" and "rounding, as far as is practicable, the sides of the train above and below, in order to offer less resistance." Calthrop acknowledged the need for removable covers to allow for ease of maintenance.

Calthrop's designs appear to have been the first to suggest a rounded, tapered-tail car for a railway train, as later used for many streamlined observation cars. While Calthrop built a model for the patent office little else resulted from his ideas during his lifetime. He eventually pursued a career as a minister for the May Memorial Unitarian Universalist Society, serving in that capacity from 1868 to 1911. It wasn't until the early 1930s that his work was rediscovered by a new generation of streamlined designers.

Frederick Upham Adams

Three decades after Calthrop, Chicago-based inventor Frederick Upham Adams pursued a remarkably similar air-resistant train design, although he professed to be ignorant of previous efforts at wind-resistant designs. Adams took a more aggressive approach in promoting his concept when he applied for a patent in 1891 (issued in 1893) and wrote a book with the weighty title *Atmospheric Resistance: Its Relation to the Speed of Railroad Trains, with an Improved System of Heating and Ventilating Cars.*

Like Calthrop, Adams was a visionary who based his aerodynamic designs on marine prototypes. There were many similarities between the two designs. The *New York Times*, writing about Adams' train on January 23, 1893, stated that "the engine . . . would be

(No Model.)

No. 489,911.

F. U. ADAMS.
RAILWAY CAR AND TRAIN.
Patented Jan. 17,

9 Sheets—

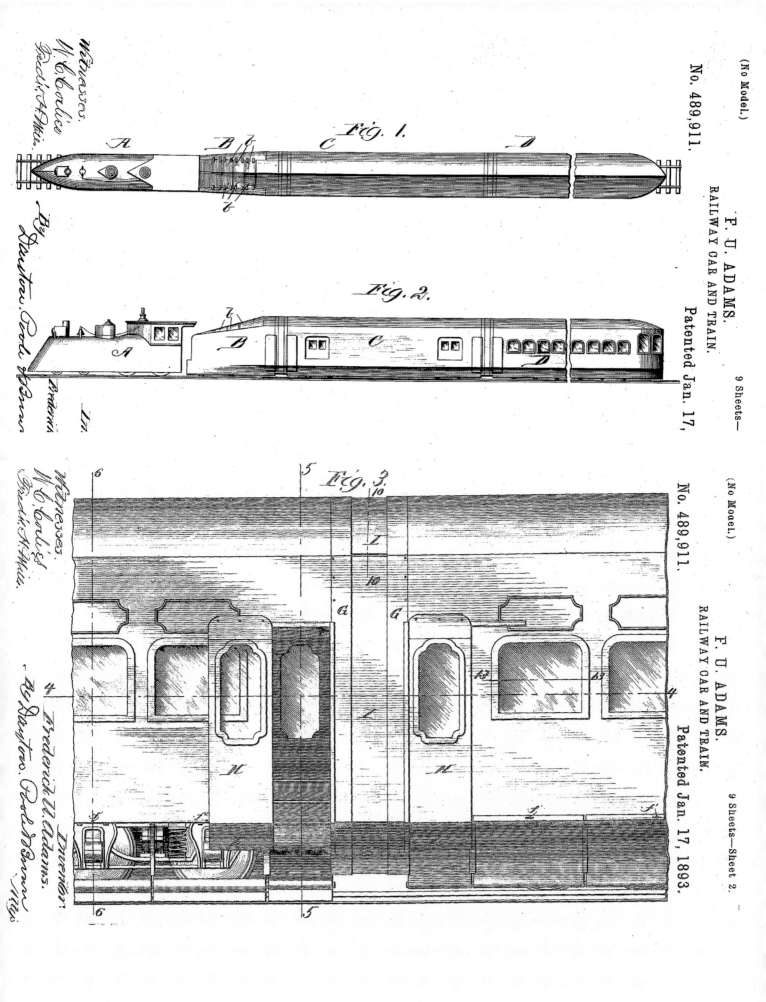

Fig. 1.

Fig. 2.

Fig. 3.

(No Model.)

No. 489,911.

F. U. ADAMS.
RAILWAY CAR AND TRAIN.
Patented Jan. 17, 1893.

9 Sheets—Sheet 2.

pointed like the bows of ship so as to split the atmosphere," while the tender would be tapered to meet the train and "vestibuled by hoods completely encircling the space between the tender and the cars. Each car of a train would thus be 'vestibuled'. A false bottom would extend beneath the cars, dropping within three inches of the track."

Adams' patent explained that his ultimate objective was to allow for trains to travel at higher speed without increased motive power, and he compared his design to "the lateral and bottom surfaces of vessels."

Adams' design approach offered much of the same wisdom of Cayley and Calthrop, as well as future practitioners of aerodynamic designs, yet in his early promotional efforts Adams' understanding of railroad dynamics appears flawed. On January 23, 1893, the *New York Times* wrote: "The present limit of express trains, Mr. Adams says, is about forty miles an hour, and those scheduled at this rate, he declares, are seldom on time." As quoted, Adams' facts were questionable. Even at that time, many trains routinely operated faster than 40 miles per hour. But more to the point, the 40-miles-per-hour operation had little to do with wind resistance, nor could reducing wind resistance have any effect on time keeping.

Adams continued to pursue his idea. In 1900, he worked with Baltimore & Ohio to build and test a prototype train. Under Adams' supervision, B&O's shops retrofitted some older passenger cars with wooden fluting, and in accordance with his earlier drawings equipped them with skirts and diaphragms between cars to reduce wind drag. The resulting train appeared remarkably similar to streamliners built thirty-five years later, except that it was hauled by an unadorned (and fairly ancient looking) 4-4-0 steam locomotive. For reasons not explained, Adams' plans for shrouding the locomotive were not embraced as part of the experiment.

On May 12, 1900, *Railway World* reported that Adams "air splitting train" was given a preliminary trial between Jersey City and Washington, DC, (using Central Railroad of New Jersey, Philadelphia & Reading, and B&O lines). Tests continued into June, but it appears that little came of the experiment, and after a while the aerodynamic fluting was removed from the cars. Adams unique train was remarkable for its early application of wind-resistant shrouds and attracted considerable attention, not just from the railroad trade press, but in the public media as well.

Pursuing Speed

Early in the twentieth century, railways in both the United States and Europe experimented with new technologies aimed at achieving higher efficiency, improved safety, and increased speed, while at the same time lowering costs.

In 1901, the 22.5-kilometer-long (13-mile) Zossen-Marienfelde military railway near Berlin was employed as the testing site for a remarkably advanced high-speed electrification experiment. This was specially wired with a high-voltage, three-phase alternating current system built by leading German electrical supply companies Siemens and Halske, and AEG. This necessitated three sets of electrical collectors mounted vertically atop the test cars. Specially equipped cars were designed for exceptionally high-speed potential.

Initial tests found that the test line itself was inadequate for the high-speed experiments, so the testing was suspended and a new, more rugged track and roadbed constructed. By October 1903, testing had resumed using modified electric cars. These were boxy in appearance and equipped with a clerestory style roof for better ventilation, but the sides of the cars were designed to minimize wind resistance. There was no mistaking these test cars for aerodynamic vehicles. They were primarily built to quantify the demands, necessities, and capabilities of electrification in high-speed service. Specifically at issue were the details of supplying current to a high-speed train, the amount of current required to reach and maintain very high speeds, and the particulars of designing equipment and track for such services. G. Freeman Allen, a British journalist noted for his writing on fast train services, noted in his book, *The Fastest Trains in the World*, "The . . . cars, quite innocent of streamlining, [were] churning up the ballast to beat a frenzied tattoo on the underside of the floor and spraying a maelstrom of flying soil and pebbles in their wake."

Although the cars were not streamlined, the Zossen speed tests carefully monitored effects and implications of air resistance. A 1905 report, translated from German and published in English by McGraw Publishing as *The Berlin-Zossen Electric Railway Tests of 1903*, detailed the test findings. The effects of wind pressure and suction around the car were measured as its speed increased. It noted that wind resistance increased dramatically as speeds climbed above 75

Built in Omaha by McKeen Motor Car Co.

miles per hour, stating at "higher speeds the resistance curves rise somewhat faster than expected."

Other experiments included attaching "pointed noses" to the front of the car, which "diminish[ed] the air resistance very considerably, for instance, at a speed of 200 km [kilometers per hour] it [was] reduced about 8 percent." The report concluded that when building a high-speed railcar, if "the most favorable form for overcoming the air resistance is used, the air resistance can be still further diminished."

Most observers were fascinated by the car's top speeds as it repeatedly surpassed 200 kilometers per hour and set a speed record for the time when it reached 210 kilometers per hour (130.5 miles per hour). Despite public awe, the Zossen tests were more than a mere spectacle and seriously demonstrated the speed potential of electric trains.

McKeen Motor Company

The first successful commercial adaptation of wind-resistant design was the work of the McKeen Motor Company prior to World War I. Its proprietor was William R. McKeen Jr., the well-educated son of an Indiana banker who interestingly had studied in Berlin in the years immediately prior to the Zossen speed

William R. McKeen was a skilled salesman and energetic entrepreneur who benefited from the vision and backing of Union Pacific godfather Edward Henry Harriman. The McKeen Motor Car Company built its cars in Union Pacific's Omaha shops. This classic McKeen "windsplitter" embraced Harriman's vision using a shiplike prow to reduce wind resistance. *Solomon collection*

tests. In 1902, he was appointed as Union Pacific's superintendent of motive power and machinery, a remarkably important post for a young man.

Railroad financier and visionary Edward Henry Harriman had taken control of Union Pacific in the late 1890s, and his administration aggressively improved the railroad using all available means, including major infrastructure projects, standardization of motive power and bridges, and widespread installation of modern electric automatic block signaling to improve capacity and safety. In 1901, Harriman took control of Southern Pacific, which not only connected with Union Pacific to form the western portion of America's premier transcontinental route, but also represented the largest transportation empire west of the Mississippi. He immediately set to work improving that property as well.

McKeen introduced the porthole windows on his seventh car built in March 1906 as Erie Railroad 4000. A vintage postcard view of Erie Railroad motorcar 4002 represents the McKeen car in its classic form, which featured porthole windows and center door. Built in 1909, Erie 4002 was McKeen's first 70-foot car, the majority of his earlier production used car bodies measuring 55 feet 2 inches long. *Solomon collection*

In 1904, Harriman asked McKeen to develop a solution to the branch line problem. Harriman, especially impressed by the recent introduction of gasoline engine–powered torpedo boats by the United States Navy, believed that internal combustion power might offer his railroad an inexpensive solution to money-losing branch line passenger operations (of which some were suffering competition from new electric, interurban trolley lines).

McKeen, like Harriman, was a maverick and uninhibited by industry prejudice. He embraced Harriman's ideas and quickly developed an economical solution based around the idea of a lightweight, wind-resistant, gasoline engine–powered railcar.

Self-propelled railcars were not a new concept and experimental steam-powered railcars dated to the 1850s, while electric trolley cars, and more recently electric multiple-units, had become standard equipment on interurban and rapid transit lines. Experiments with gasoline engine cars dated to 1888 when William Patton of Pueblo, Colorado, dabbled with a gas-mechanical car. He didn't have luck with its mechanical transmission and began developing gasoline-electric cars in 1890.

However, at the time McKeen took the reins of Harriman's project, there were no commercially successful internal combustion engine railcars being manufactured in the United States. McKeen elevated this concept to a new level and created, what John H. White Jr. described in *The American Passenger Car*, "one of the most distinctive and imaginative rail vehicles ever produced."

Not only did McKeen's unusual blend of aerodynamic design and internal combustion power foretell development of true streamlined trains three decades later, but his efforts directly inspired two of the principle players of the 1930s streamlined train design. Arthur H. Fetters and Edward G. Budd both worked closely with McKeen. Fetters continued to work for Union Pacific, where he was closely involved in the railroad's early internal combustion investigations in the 1920s, and its diesel and streamlining projects of the 1930s, while Budd's association with McKeen contributed to his later success as streamlined train pioneer and railcar manufacturer, discussed in the following paragraphs and in Chapter 2.

As the case with other early aerodynamic designs, McKeen's wind-resistant shapes originated with nautical designs and clearly emulated the naval torpedo boats that had inspired Harriman in the first place. McKeen's first car was a single-truck experimental prototype using a wooden body built in early 1905. His second prototype was constructed in September of that year and used a steel truss design that set important precedents for his later production.

In 1905 McKeen applied for a patent (issued in 1910) that outlined the basic premises for his cars. His design incorporated truss framing, similar to bridge construction, which enabled "simple and light construction" that possessed maximum strength and rigidity. The shape of the carbody frame aimed to reduce air resistance to a minimum and thus increase the "tractive power without increasing weight." Lastly, his design aimed to preserve the shape of the car "in the face of all stresses brought to bear thereon in the course of hard, practical use."

His patent indicated that aerodynamic design had two key purposes: to improve adhesion and reduce wind drag. During experiments, McKeen noticed that misdirected wind pressure had the tendency to lift the car from the track resulting in a loss of tractive power. His design was intended to do the opposite; McKeen

Jamestown, Chautauqua & Lake Erie car No. 1, pictured at Chautauqua, New York, is an example of a 55-foot car built by McKeen in 1911. McKeen was an early proponent of wind-resistant design, however his concept of a knife-edged "prow" with a rounded end was the reverse of true aerodynamic theory. Despite McKeen's advocacy of wind resistance, few of his cars traveled fast enough for the shape to affect performance. *Solomon collection*

noted "the entire outer surface is so formed as to utilize the wind pressure in driving the car toward the track." The second feature was aimed at reducing forward wind resistance with the knife-edge prow, while "the general spheroidal shape of the rear end of the frame" prevented a partial vacuum from forming at the back of the car.

According to White, in the 1907 *Railway Review* McKeen explained that his "wedge-shaped front" was the result of experiments in Germany (likely the Zossen speed trials) and demonstrations with an electric railcar at the 1904 St. Louis Louisiana Purchase Exposition. White further notes that McKeen claimed "a car with a flat front was subjected to wind resistance equal to 87.5 horsepower, while resistance to the wedge front amounted to only 21.9 horsepower." While McKeen's source for this data is a mystery, his intent demonstrates that he followed a wind-resistant approach in his car design. As it turns out, from the point of view of actually reducing wind resistance, his cars were operated incorrectly, that is back to front. Later wind-tunnel experiments confirmed that

continued on page 24

McKeen didn't limit production to rail vehicles; he also produced autobuses using similar advanced construction techniques. How would you like to ride on unimproved Minnesota roads in this contraption? Rail travel still seemed like a good option by comparison. *Solomon collection*

Opposite top: Today, the McKeen car looks ancient, but in the early twentieth century it was seen as futuristic and modern. Some observers objected to its nautical appearance, while many riders found its gasoline engine too loud. This McKeen motor car built in 1914 was advertised as "The latest thing in railroad equipment." It served the Central New York Southern between Auburn and Ithaca, New York; seated eighty-three people; and, using a 200-horsepower engine, was capable of 70 miles per hour. *Solomon collection*

Opposite bottom: Harriman-controlled Union Pacific and Southern Pacific were the largest buyers of McKeen's windsplitters. More than 150 cars were built in Omaha between 1905 and 1917. Significantly, the cars embodied some principles of aerodynamic design and were powered by internal combustion engines, two of the key elements of Union Pacific's streamlined trains developed a generation later. *Solomon collection*

NOW IN USE ON THE "SHORT LINE" BETWEEN AUBURN AND ITHACA, N.Y.

1365. Motor Car Used on the Southern Pacific Lines in Oregon.

"ON THE LINE OF A THOUSAND WONDERS."

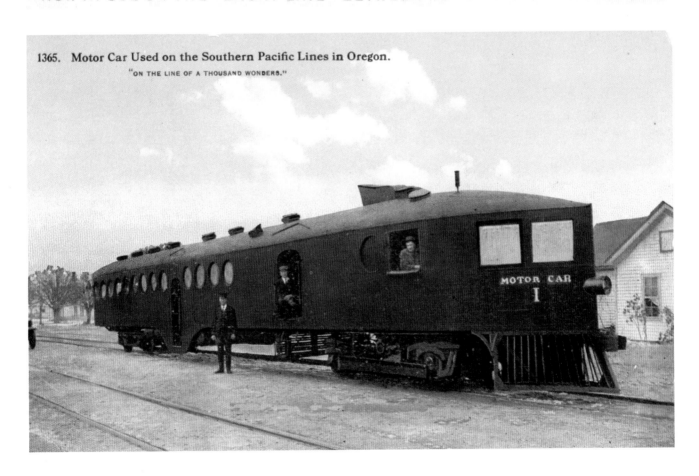

McKeen's 1910 patent for car body construction displays the most common arrangement for his motor cars with porthole windows and a center door. *United States Patent No. 973,366, Oct.18, 1910*

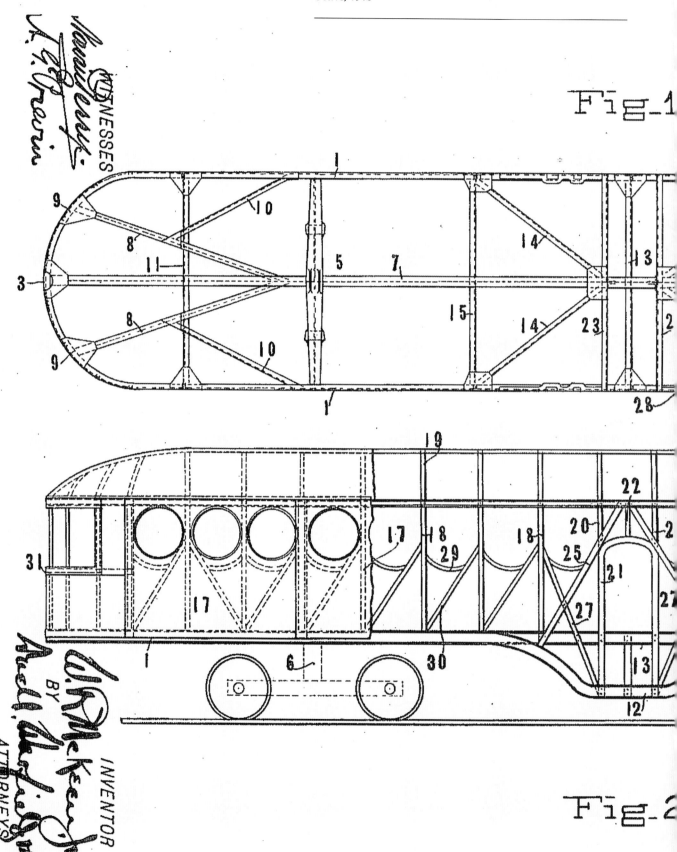

Fig_1

Fig_2

973,366.

W. R. McKEEN, Jr.
CAR BODY CONSTRUCTION.
APPLICATION FILED JAN. 17, 1907.

Patented Oct. 18, 1910.
2 SHEETS—SHEET 2.

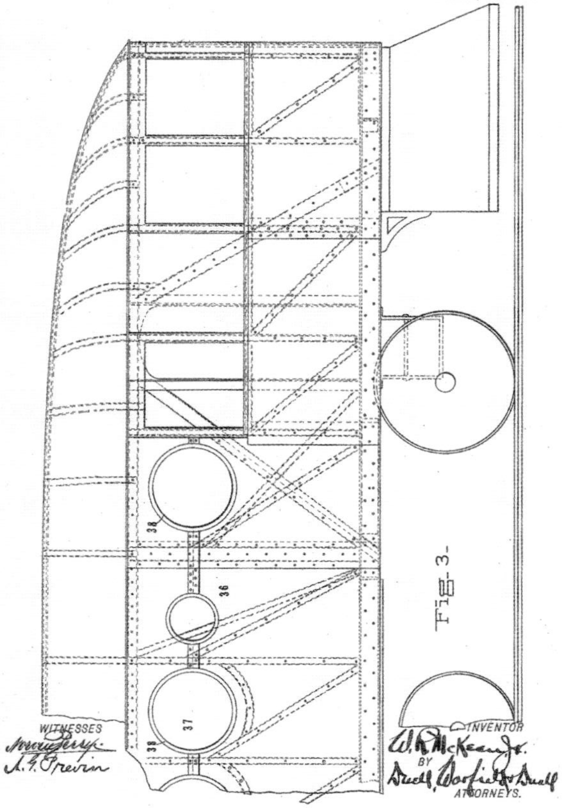

973,366.

W. R. McKEEN, Jr.
CAR BODY CONSTRUCTION.
APPLICATION FILED JAN. 17, 1907.

Patented Oct. 18, 1910
2 SHEETS—SHEET 1.

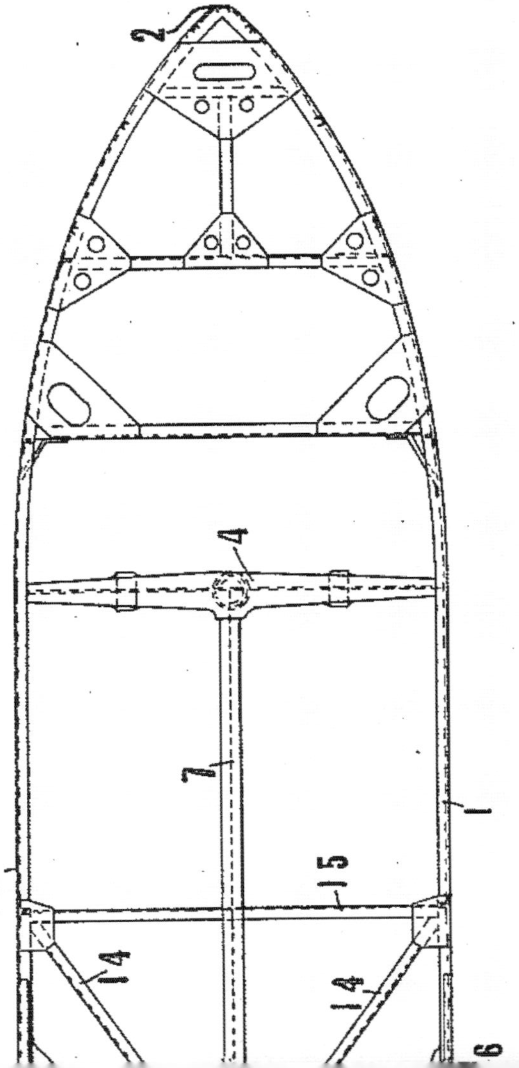

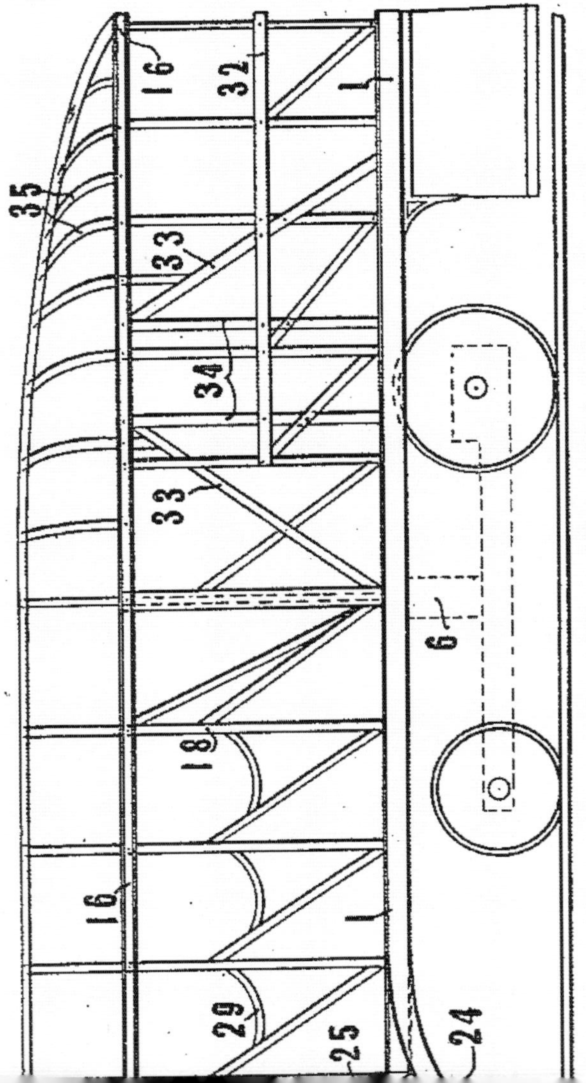

Fig. 3.

continued from page 20
a parabolic front end and a tapered back end greatly lowered wind resistance.

The nature of the truss construction demanded relatively small windows, and in 1906 McKeen's seventh car introduced porthole windows, a feature that would be a defining characteristic of most of his subsequent production, which included unpowered trailers, at least one electric car, and a limited excursion into automotive buses for highway transport.

McKeen moved quickly, taking his patents and radical concepts into a commercial business constructing and selling lightweight, high-speed, steel-bodied, gasoline-powered, self-propelled railcars. In 1907, with Harriman's approval and investment, McKeen set up a commercial venture to build and market gasoline railcars. In *Interurbans without Wires*, Edmund Keilty explains that Harriman allocated UP's North Shop complex in Omaha for McKeen's enterprise, which continued to benefit from significant orders from Harriman's UP and SP and affiliated lines, as well as the professional backing of Harriman who was one of the great players in American railroading. The McKeen Motor Car Company was officially launched on July 1, 1908.

While he had some competition, notably from General Electric, McKeen Company remained a significant gas car producer and built more than 150 cars over a dozen years from the time of his initial prototypes. E. H. Harriman died in September 1909, but McKeen continued to sell cars to a variety of railroads in the United States, as well as companies in Australia, Canada, Cuba, and Mexico. Yet his venture has not been viewed as a commercial success.

The McKeen cars were plagued with mechanical problems, many stemming from his primitive engine designs and ineffective transmission system. Other than the Harriman roads, he enjoyed very few repeat customers, and orders for new cars dwindled rapidly after 1912. The onset of World War I sealed the fate of the company. The last cars were delivered in 1917, and in 1920 Union Pacific assumed the McKeen company's remaining assets.

Other companies went on to perfect gas electric cars after World War I. Ultimately McKeen's influence was far more important than the cars he built in the early years of the twentieth century. Although commercially

Opposite: Paul Jaray was a design engineer at the Zeppelin works at Freidrichshafen, Germany, and a pioneer using wind-tunnel tests to perfect aerodynamic shapes. His streamlined automobile of 1922 reversed the teardrop shape that McKeen adopted for his railway Motor Car two decades earlier. *United States Patent No. 1,631,269, June 7, 1927*

unsuccessful, McKeen's futuristic "wind-splitters" are considered a precursor to the streamlined styling of the 1930s. Not only did he help pave the way for the use of internal combustion engines for railway motive power, but his innovative car design inspired significant developments decades later that were key to America's first commercial streamlined trains. And this was no coincidence. As mentioned earlier, Edward G. Budd, one of the most significant pioneers of streamlined lightweight design, was closely involved in construction of the McKeen cars.

In his two-part article published in *Railroad History* issues 172 and 173 in 1995, Mark Reutter detailed Budd's connections to McKeen and other industry suppliers. In the early years of the twentieth century, Budd was employed by Hale & Kilburn, supplier of seats and railcar components to Pullman and other passenger car builders. Budd specialized in pressed-steel construction and industrial strength welding, relatively new fields where few had experience. Growing safety concerns in the railcar industry during its fundamental transitional period from traditional wooden-bodied cars to all-steel construction made his experience useful, which is why McKeen had taken interest in Budd's work in the first place. McKeen contracted H&K to produce his rail carbodies, taking advantage of Budd's stamped- and pressed-steel skills, key to McKeen's pioneering railcar designs using heretofore untried contours.

Budd quit H&K in 1912 to start his Edward G. Budd Manufacturing Company. He continued to develop his innovative manufacturing processes, initially focusing on welded-steel automotive bodies. In the 1920s, Budd's fascination with modern alloyed steels fueled refinement of his proprietary "shot-welding" process for stainless steel. This led to his renewed interest in lightweight railcar construction in the 1930s followed by the Burlington's *Zephyr* detailed in Chapter 2.

June 7, 1927.

P. JARAY

1,631,269

MOTOR CAR

Filed Aug. 19 1922

2 Sheets-Sheet 1

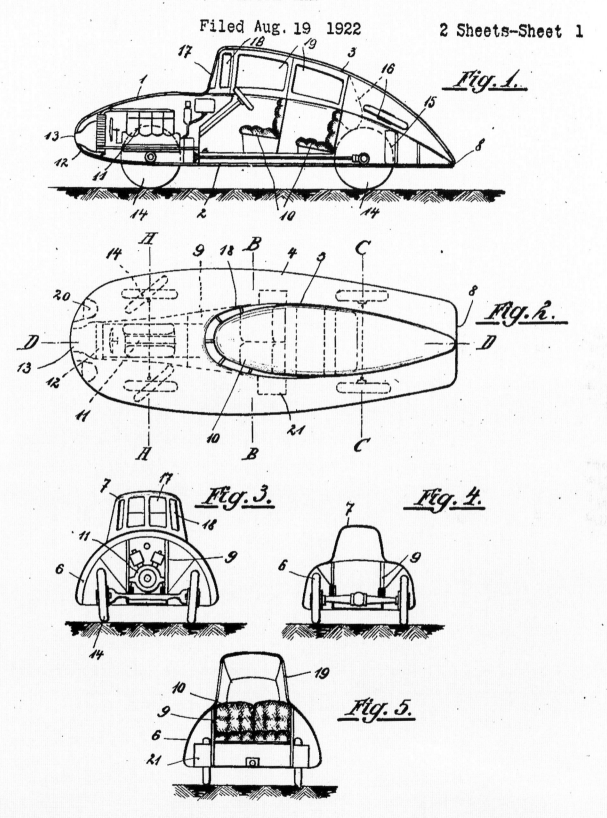

Fig. 1.

Fig. 2.

Fig. 3.

Fig. 4.

Fig. 5.

Inventor:

Paul Jaray

6 · 1835 – 1935 · 100 Jahre · Deutsche Eisenbahn · 6 · Deutsches Reich

12 · 1835 – 1935 · 100 Jahre · Deutsche Eisenbahn · 12 · Deutsches Reich

25 · 1835 – 1935 · 100 Jahre · Deutsche Eisenbahn · 25 · Deutsches Reich

40 · 1835 – 1935 · 100 Jahre · Deutsche Eisenbahn · 40 · Deutsches Reich

CHAPTER 2

NEW MATERIALS AND NEW MODES

Advanced aerodynamic designs were spurred by the rise of both the automotive and aeronautical industries during World War I. Innovation and research into new materials and manufacturing techniques continued into the 1920s, with technological advances in America developed in parallel with similar trends in Germany and Britain. Metallurgical research produced new lightweight steel and aluminum alloys. New methods of working with these materials enabled much lighter construction and allowed for new vehicle shapes that changed the way designers thought about construction. While innovative automobile and aircraft design led the way, it didn't take long before railway suppliers adapted these techniques for experimental applications.

Significantly, these new techniques coincided with an aesthetic revolution. The postwar generation rejected the intricate ornate elegance that characterized architecture and machinery of the nineteenth and early twentieth centuries. Designers now prized smooth surfaces and "clean-lined" shapes, such as those promoted by the German Bauhaus movement. Bright colors replaced sedate darker shades; soft, indirect lighting took the place of direct lighting; and

compound curves were used instead of the blunt utility of older harsh-angled designs.

However, while automotive and aircraft manufacturers were new industries and embraced innovation, the railroad industry was well established, set in its ways, and saddled by a culture that discouraged innovative practices and new technology. If it weren't for desperate financial conditions caused by the Great Depression, combined with the rapid erosion of railroad traffic by other modes, railroads would have likely continued to ignore the technological advances developed by their competition. The Depression encouraged American railroads to embrace change, and experiment, embrace, and implement new designs to create bold new trains.

Lightweight train design, internal combustion propulsion, and aerodynamic design were three distinct technological movements for railroad design at the time. These were combined in various ways, along with modern styling, to produce families of new streamlined trains.

The streamlined era flourished on both sides of the Atlantic from the mid-1930s onward, with railways on both continents learning and adapting each other's ideas in a variety of ways. While American firms experimented and innovated, they also borrowed ideas and technology from their European counterparts.

Germany's Flying Hamburger

Germany's early twentieth-century interest in high-speed train design proved a driving force for the development of key technologies coalescing in the

Opposite: In 1935, special-issue German stamps, issued during the Nazi era, commemorated 100 years of German railways. At the bottom, modern streamlined trains included Flying Hamburger diesel railcars at left and a streamlined 4-6-2 Pacific (right) in contrast with *Der Adler* (the Eagle), the first locomotive to operate on German rails (top left). *Hundert Jahre Deutsche Eisenbahnen, Solomon collection*

Right: Germany's *Schienenzeppelin* (Rail Zeppelin) was a unique high-speed experimental train. Developed in 1929, this was one of the first modern rail-vehicles designed in a wind tunnel. Although it demonstrated fantastic land speed—a reported 143 miles per hour—the car was entirely impractical for revenue service. *Solomon collection*

Below right: In 1932, Wagen und Maschinenbau AG built a streamlined, two-piece articulated, diesel-electric railcar powered by a pair of twelve-cylinder, 410-horsepower Maybach diesel engines. *Hundert Jahre Deutsche Eisenbahnen, Solomon collection*

early 1930s with the first successful streamlined, aerodynamic trains. Aerodynamic design, combined with modern automotive and aircraft manufacturing technologies, produced a radical new type of train: the diesel streamliner. Its success encouraged similar efforts across Europe and in America.

As highlighted in Chapter 1, Germany set railway land speed records with its Berlin–Zossen speed tests in 1903, using a boxy, electrically powered vehicle. During the 1920s, German engineers pioneered advances in aerodynamic automotive designs and small diesel-powered railcars. By 1930, Germany's innovative aerodynamic design produced a freakish combination of aircraft and railway technology called the *Schienenzeppelin* (the famous "Rail Zeppelin"). This bizarre-looking machine, an experimental propeller-powered railcar designed for exceptionally fast running, is understood to have

reached 143 miles per hour (230 kilometers per hour) in tests.

Like many early superfast trains, *Schienenzeppelin* wasn't practical for revenue service, yet it spurred further German design efforts to develop a practical high-speed train. Key to this work were advances in diesel propulsion that made possible compact high-output engines, combined with aerodynamic streamlining and lightweight train fabrication using aircraft- and automotive-style construction.

In 1932, Wagen und Maschinenbau AG built the world's first high-speed diesel train using an articulated, two-piece, streamlined diesel-electric railcar powered by a pair of twelve-cylinder, 410-horsepower Maybach diesel engines. Its aerodynamic design was based on experiences with the Rail Zeppelin. The Zeppelin Works on the shore of Lake Constance at Friedrichshafen were used for wind-tunnel experiments to design new shapes for reducing air drag. Although not the first time a wind tunnel had been used for railway experiments, it was among the earliest practical rail wind-tunnel applications.

The novel use of diesel propulsion and a sleek aerodynamic body made the train newsworthy. Yet making the train functional required significant development of subsidiary technologies. Advanced braking technology and improved signaling were necessary for the train to work safely on existing railway lines.

The new streamlined train was carefully tested before entering regular service on the Deutsche Reichsbahn (German State Railways) on May 15, 1933, as the *Fliegende Hamburger* ("The Flying Hamburger"), running between Berlin and Hamburg. While the Berlin–Hamburg run had long been a fast route and was characterized by lots of level tangent track, the new train caught the attention of railways everywhere because it now was the fastest regularly scheduled train in the world. In 2 hours 18 minutes the new diesel train covered a 178-mile (270 kilometer) run, traveling at an average start-to-stop speed of 77.4 miles per hour (125 kilometers per hour). To maintain this fast average speed required long stretches of sustained 100 miles per hour (160 kilometers per hour) running.

Significantly, the *Fliegende Hamburger* dramatically outpaced steam schedules and encouraged a host of similar German diesel trains while inspiring comparable efforts across Western Europe and in America.

On the heels of this success, Deutsche Reichsbahn ordered seventeen additional diesel streamlined trains to create a network of high-speed services linking most major German cities. Of these, thirteen trains were two-unit sets based on the prototype, while four featured three-piece articulated sets. Two of the three-piece sets featured a hydraulic transmission system that set a precedent for later diesel locomotive development in Germany.

By 1935, Deutsche Reichsbahn's streamlined railcars were operating twelve of the world's swiftest schedules. Although the trains were enormously successful with the traveling public, they served during one of the darkest periods of Germany's history and services were suspended with the advent of World War II. Surviving high-speed trains worked after the war in both East and West Germany, and after withdrawal from regular traffic a few of these pioneering trains

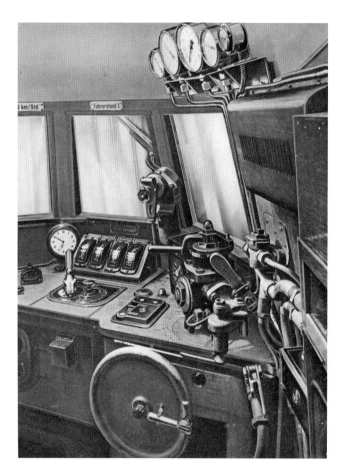

Drivers' controls for a high-speed German diesel-electric railcar of the variety assigned to Flying Hamburger services. *Hundert Jahre Deutsche Eisenbahnen, Solomon collection*

were preserved; the original *Fliegende Hamburger* is displayed at the Verkehrsmuseum in Nürnberg (Nuremburg Transport Museum).

Electro-Motive and General Motors

In the early 1920s, forward-thinking entrepreneur Harold L. Hamilton combined his knowledge of railroad technology with his skills as a highway motor truck salesman to capitalize on a resurgent gas-electric railcar market. On August 31, 1922, Hamilton and his business partner, Paul Turner, formed the Cleveland, Ohio–based Electro-Motive Engineering Corporation (soon renamed the Electro-Motive Company).

Their business methods were unusual: they recruited gas-electric specialists and used nonconventional approaches to sales and production. Instead of custom designing cars for individual customers and manufacturing the cars themselves, EMC produced standard designs and coordinated subcontractors for

Above & Opposite: One of several surviving German DVT 877 high-speed railcars in its classic navy and cream livery was displayed at the Leipzig Haupbahnhof in June 2001. Built in the early 1930s, these were the first aerodynamic high-speed railcars and set important design precedents for both European and American trains. There are numerous functional similarities between the German *Fliegende Hamburger* (Flying Hamburger) trains and early American streamliners. *Brian Solomon*

manufacturing and assembly. Soon they were building the best gas-electric railcars in America. These well-engineered, dependable cars quickly earned EMC a loyal customer base among the large railroads, including Chicago, Burlington & Quincy (Burlington), and Atchison, Topeka & Santa Fe (Santa Fe), which later would invest in EMC's earliest diesel-powered streamliners.

EMC's low-cost, reliable cars not only advanced the company's reputation, but allowed it to perfect internal combustion/electric technologies, which put it on the path toward development of mainline diesel-electric locomotives. While its early cars were small and operated singly, it gradually developed larger and more powerful cars.

The Great Depression forever changed EMC and its business in ways that no one could have anticipated. First the economic downturn devastated the rail-car market. Then in 1930, automotive giant General Motors opted to acquire EMC's primary engine supplier, the Winton engine company, a move followed by its acquisition of EMC itself.

As a GM subsidiary, Electro-Motive Company was renamed Electro-Motive Corporation. This move set the stage for the most dramatic advances in American motive power and train design during the twentieth century. Despite the economic austerity of the early Depression years, General Motors infused capital and resources into EMC and Winton that allowed for research, design, and production of internal combustion–powered streamlined trains that set new patterns for American train design.

Railroads Face Economic Turmoil

The effects of World War I had clogged the North American railroad network with traffic that resulted in a controversial period of government control. After the war, the railroads were returned to their owners but immediately faced rapidly expanding highway and

Pullman's pioneering *Railplane* of 1933 is displayed at Chicago & North Western terminal. This demonstrated the advantages of lightweight aircraft-style body construction, aerodynamic design, and structural aluminum as applied to a railway vehicle. *J. Michael Gruber collection*

air competition because the war had accelerated development of those industries. Cars, buses, and trucks eroded railroad market share and earnings during the 1920s, yet because the economy was robust overall, railroad traffic remained strong.

However, onset of the Depression quickly devastated traffic levels and forced railroads to retrench. Branch lines were hard hit, which rapidly dried up the market for gas-electric cars. By 1933, mainline freight traffic had declined sharply, while long-distance

passenger numbers had cascaded downward to modern lows. Action was needed to rejuvenate the industry.

Pullman and the *Railplane*

By the 1920s, Pullman-Standard was the best-known manufacturer of railroad passenger cars. Founded by Mortimer Pullman in the 1860s, the company had grown and developed its business starting with long-distance sleeping cars to include a whole spectrum of railway vehicles. In 1927, Pullman became the primary car supplier for EMC, which forged an important link between the two companies.

Pullman also made two significant independent forays into railcar design. As Edmund Keilty profiled Pullman's railcar production in *Interurbans without Wires*: in 1925, the company built a pair of

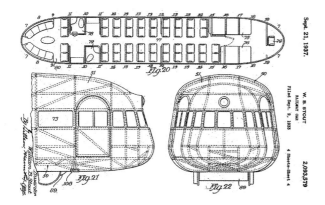

Sept. 21, 1937.   W. B. STOUT   2,093,579   RAILWAY CAR   Filed Sept. 2, 1933   4 Sheets-Sheet 4

William B. Stout's patent for Pullman's experimental *Railplane* was filed on September 2, 1933, and awarded a little more than four years later. Although the train was never replicated, it set precedents that were incorporated in later Pullman streamliners and represents an important step in the streamlined design that culminated in Electro-Motive's postwar E- and F-units. *United States Patent No. 2093579, September 21, 1937*

conventionally appearing gas-electrics for Henry Ford's Detroit, Toledo & Ironton line. While by no means streamlined, these cars made significant use of aluminum to reduce weight, and Keilty suggests that Ford engineers may have been involved in their design.

Seven years later, in 1932, Pullman engineered a far more innovative experimental railcar using modern lightweight tubular design and largely aluminum construction featuring a sleek aerodynamic body style. Named the *Railplane*, this was in effect a literal translation of aircraft design for a railway application. It was the work of William B. Stout (see sidebar on page 40), known for his design of Ford's Tri-Motor aircraft, and featured a welded tubular frame with a riveted aluminum skin. Measuring 60 feet long and weighing just 12.5 tons, it was substantially lighter per passenger than a conventional railcar. A lighter train would cost less to power than a heavier one, so lightweight design was seen as key to operating at much faster speeds.

The *Railplane* was built at Pullman's expense at a time of exceptional austerity in the railway supply industry, and Pullman hoped that this radical adaptation of aircraft design might intrigue railroads and stimulate sales. It was one of the earliest modern examples of a streamlined railway vehicle for use on an American steam railway.

John H. White Jr., in *The American Railroad Passenger Car*, detailed the *Railplane*, highlighting its distinctive design and its testing on Gulf, Mobile & Northern in September 1932—an experiment that coincided with similar tests with the *Fliegende Hamburger* in Germany. On at least one occasion the *Railplane* hit 90 miles per hour.

Century of Progress

In 1933, Chicago's Century of Progress Exposition was a seminal event that spurred the synergy of diesel-power, streamlining, and lightweight train construction. None of the concepts was totally new to American railroads, but they hadn't yet caught national interest: since the end of World War I, American railways had dabbled with diesel power, while the Budd Company had experimented with European technologies and Pullman experimented with lightweight train designs.

By 1933, the world had taken notice of Germany's successful *Fliegende Hamburger*, and some American businessmen wondered if they too could build lightweight, high-speed streamlined diesel trains.

Among the exhibits were Pullman's *Railplane* and Winton's compact experimental 201 diesel engine. The event brought together key railroad leaders, industry innovators and inventors, and larger manufacturers resulting in the design and production of two distinct streamlined trains: Union Pacific's M-10000 and Burlington's *Zephyr*. Interestingly, both trains had personal connections to the McKeen cars of the previous generation (see Chapter 1).

Union Pacific's *Streamliner*

W. Averell Harriman was Union Pacific's Chairman and grandson of the late E. H Harriman. The elder Harriman had been one of the great railroad moguls of the late nineteenth and early twentieth centuries, and who a generation earlier had encouraged McKeen to develop his wind-splitters. So, through its affiliations with McKeen, Union Pacific was among the earliest proponents of internal combustion high-speed train design.

In his history of Union Pacific, Maury Klein points out that Averell Harriman arranged for Arthur H. Fetters (McKeen's former assistant) to visit Europe in 1926 to investigate diesel engine developments. As a result, Fetters was part of the direct trans-Atlantic technology transfer during the inter-war period. The Depression encouraged Harriman to fund high-speed train development in hopes that a sexy new train would awe the public while cutting transit times. Klein *continued on page 36*

Union Pacific's original M-10000 three-piece articulated streamlined train at Pullman's Chicago plant in 1934. Like its *Railplane* of 1933, William B. Stout of Stout Engineering Laboratories, Dearborn, Michigan, designed this for Pullman. *J. Michael Gruber collection*

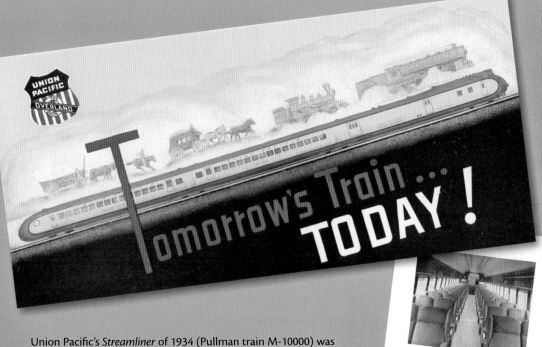

Union Pacific's *Streamliner* of 1934 (Pullman train M-10000) was designed to awe passengers. This brochure displayed the features and style of the new train, explaining that "every effort has been made in its building to provide travel pleasure." The train entered service as *City of Salina* (Kansas City to Salina, Kansas), which was a relatively minor run compared with Union Pacific's transcontinental services. *Union Pacific brochure, Solomon collection*

Looking Toward Rear of Last Car.

MODERN ART entered the field of rail car construction on Union Pacific's new train. The exterior is an unusual blending of golden brown and canary yellow separated by a narrow red stripe which extends the entire length of the train and accentuates the stream-lined effect. The interior is striking in its simplicity. The color scheme is blue, shading down from a nearly white ceiling, through the lighter shades of blue to a dark blue below the window sills. There are horizontal bands of polished aluminum showing between the different shades of blue. Window sills are black bake-lite. The chairs are trimmed in aluminum and the seats are upholstered in a golden brown tapestry. The floor has a harmoniously colored aisle strip. Window shades are a Venetian blind design and curtain rollers are entirely concealed. The simplicity of the entire decorative scheme creates a pleasing atmosphere of restful beauty.

A second train, incorporating sleeping cars, is under construction.

TRAVEL COMFORT
has been given a
NEW SIGNIFICANCE

WESTERN travelers of tomorrow will enjoy comforts and conveniences heretofore unknown—the result of innovations in design and construction introduced by Union Pacific in its new high-speed, light-weight, stream-lined train. The train is fully air-conditioned, thus eliminating all draught and dirt. The seats for 116 passengers in the two coaches of the train were especially designed for this equipment. A novel device makes it possible to install individual tables at each seat for service of meals from the buffet or for use as a writing desk. Meals, prepared in the unique buffet kitchen, will be served from special combination tea-cart steam table by waiters who pass through the aisles. Windows, all of shatter-proof glass, were manufactured under a special formula to fake the glare out of sunlight. An indirect lighting system insures uniform light without shadows. Comfort, convenience and beauty of design are apparent in every feature of the entire train. Every effort has been made in its building to provide travel pleasure in Union Pacific's new train.

The Buffet — in Rear of Last Car.

UNION PACIFIC *Pioneer*

"The exect board of dire the conclusic the development of a railway

Here is a completely new type of railway in color harmonies, and preeminent in utility, convenience and

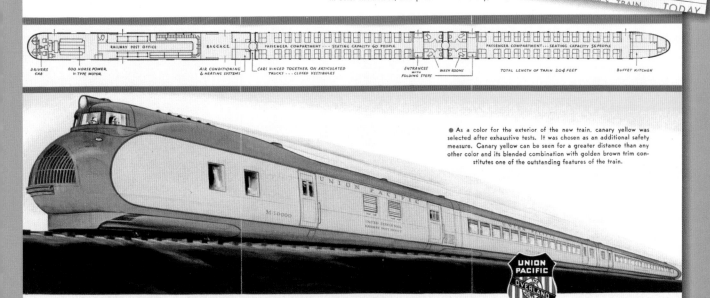

● As a color for the exterior of the new train, canary yellow was selected after exhaustive tests. It was chosen as an additional safety measure. Canary yellow can be seen for a greater distance than any other color and its blended combination with golden brown trim constitutes one of the outstanding features of the train.

SUPER SPEED—WITH SAFETY—AND COMFORT

PROGRESS

"THE LAUREL WREATH FOR TRANSPORTATION PROGRESS MUST GO TO THE UNION PACIFIC RAILROAD"

—George Creel in Collier's, August 5, 1933

UNION PACIFIC

Above: Success of the original M-10000 immediately led Union Pacific to order additional Pullman streamliners. Similar in appearance to M-10000 was the diesel-powered M-10001, shown on the cover of UP's *Progress* brochure. This featured a longer, heavier consist that was designed for long-distance overnight travel. *Solomon collection*

Below: Key to the lightweight design of Pullman's M-10000 was its aluminum construction. Alcoa Aluminum issued special all-aluminum tokens to commemorate its role in production of the new train. However, high-aluminum content contributed to UP's decision to scrap the train during World War II when the metal was highly valued for the war effort. *Solomon collection*

continued from page 33

notes that the railroad initiated a program in 1932 to produce a "Super Train" that would curb long distance passenger declines by cutting one day out of its fastest transcontinental schedules.

Harriman was impressed by Pullman's *Railplane* displays, so he wasted little time in pushing this train design to the next level. On May 23, 1933, he made an official statement explaining, "The executive officers of the Union Pacific several months ago reached the conclusion that to save and restore passenger business to the rails would necessitate the development of a radically different type of passenger equipment."

The following day, the railroad ordered a three-piece high-speed train from Pullman, known as the M-10000 (McKeen's experimental railcar had begun with his M-1). While an advancement and a practical application of the *Railplane* concept, this embraced a number of significant design changes.

The M-10000's aerodynamic design, like the *Railplane*, was engineered by Stout. The body was constructed from aluminum using advanced aircraft-style tubular framing with riveted sheet-metal skin designed by Pullman's Martin Blomberg. The train featured a low-profile, low-center-of-gravity body shape that was 3 feet shorter than a typical heavyweight passenger

Left: Period postcard view of Union Pacific's *City of Portland* Pullman train M-10001. The forward-facing grille that characterized Union Pacific streamliners had a tendency to collect debris as the train raced along. Later designs relocated air vents to the side of the locomotive. *Solomon collection*

Below: The early Pullman trains with their forward-facing grilles were reportedly a nightmare to clean; dead birds and debris would collect in the engine compartment during their high-speed cross-country dashes. Later designs featured side air-intakes. In 1936, the Pullman-built M-10001 assigned to *City of Portland* service rests at Chicago & North Western's Chicago coach yards during a layover. This diesel train delivered a significantly faster schedule than long-distance steam-powered trains. *Jay Williams collection*

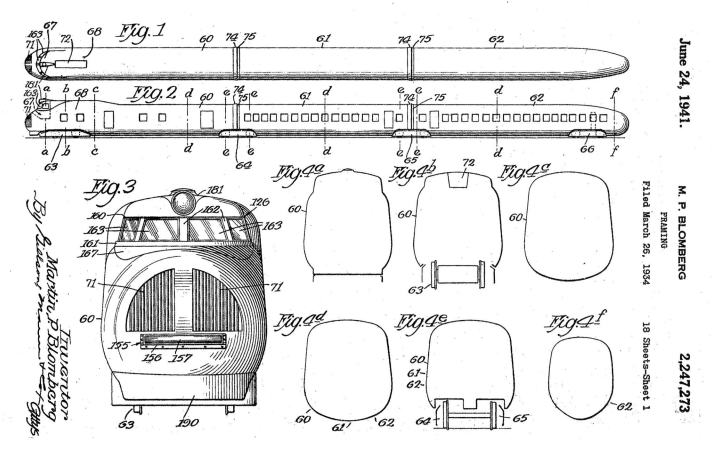

June 24, 1941.

M. P. BLOMBERG

FRAMING

Filed March 26, 1934   18 Sheets-Sheet 1

2,247,273

Martin Blomberg was awarded this patent for the structure of Pullman's original three-car M-10000. Blomberg worked for Pullman for ten years before continuing his work on streamlined train design for General Motors Electro-Motive Corporation in 1935. Although rarely acknowledged for his work, Blomberg's structural designs were among the most influential of the streamlined era. *United States Patent No. 2,247,273, June 24, 1941*

car of the period and rode just a few inches above the rail head. However, to meet concerns for crash-worthiness, the M-10000 was more sturdily built than the *Railplane*. The result was that although the M-10000 was substantially lighter than a conventional heavyweight train, it didn't achieve the exceptionally light aircraftlike passenger-to-vehicle weight ratio offered by its experimental predecessor.

More significantly, instead of simply a single car, the M-10000—initially named the *Streamliner*—was a three-piece articulated trainset. It was impressive looking and featured the driver's cab perched above the engine compartment with a large forward-facing, two-piece grille that looked like an angry, gaping mouth. Articulation between the cars reduced weight, allowing adjacent cars to use a hinged arrangement sharing one common truck between them. This also contributed to a smoother ride at high speeds because fixed coupling and shared trucks minimize slack

action and thus ameliorated shocks when accelerating or decelerating.

Electro-Motive was closely involved with the project, and it is understood that initially Union Pacific hoped to power the train with one of Winton's new 201 diesels. However, that diesel engine was months away from practical application, so a Winton 600-horsepower distillate spark plug engine powered the M-10000 instead. This may have seemed like a nominal difference when the stunning new train debuted, but it deprived it from the significant title as America's *first* diesel streamlined train. Had no competing train been built, UP's *Streamliner* may have remained the most amazing train on American rails.

Opposite above: Blomberg's structural innovations enabled the construction of a very strong lightweight train using a modern aerodynamic shape that was conceived using wind-tunnel experiments with scale models. Blomberg assigned his patents to Pullman. *United States Patent No. 2,247,273, June 24, 1941*

Opposite below: In the 1930s Blomberg continued to refine his designs: this patent reflects innovations introduced on Pullman's second Union Pacific streamliner, train M-10001, which were intended to lower the center-of-gravity of the diesel engine while properly distributing weight to the driving wheels and to allow easy access to machinery for inspection and maintenance. *United States Patent No. 2,079,748, May 11, 1937*

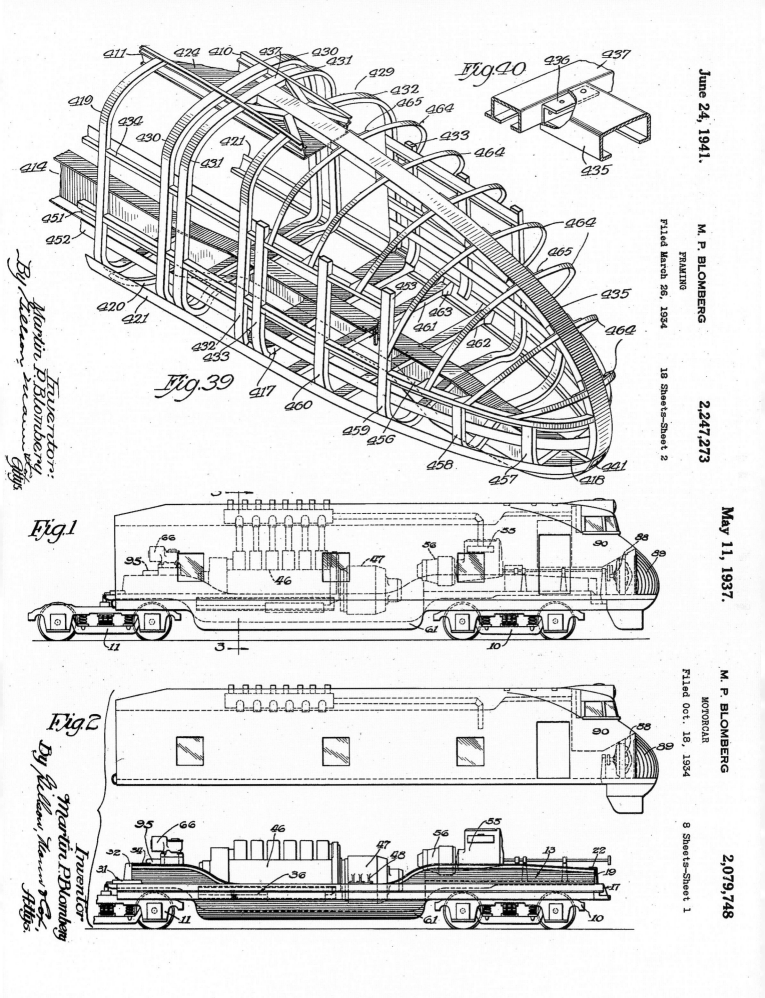

June 24, 1941.   M. P. BLOMBERG   2,247,273

FRAMING

Filed March 26, 1934   18 Sheets-Sheet 2

Fig.40

Fig.39

Inventor:
Martin P. Blomberg
By

Attys.

May 11, 1937.   M. P. BLOMBERG   2,079,748

MOTORCAR

Filed Oct. 18, 1934   8 Sheets-Sheet 1

Fig.1

Fig.2

Inventor
Martin P. Blomberg
By

Attys.

WILLIAM B. STOUT

by John Gruber

Automotive designer William B. Stout (1880–1956) of Stout Engineering Laboratories, Dearborn, Michigan, was responsible for early-1930s streamlined trainsets built by Pullman. Stout had a brief but productive relationship with the car builder, resulting in the *Railplane* (1933), Union Pacific M-10000, the first streamliner (1934), M-10001, *City of Portland* (1935), and the IC's *Green Diamond* (1936).

Stout's unusual work attracted *Popular Mechanics*, which featured the *Railplane* on the cover and in a four-page article, "Air-Minded Railroading." Stout wrote that "it is the product of aeronautical designers, engineers, and mechanics and, since it closely resembles an airplane, without wings, propeller or tail assembly, it is called the Railplane." It was designed under a contract with Pullman. "I am convinced that we stand on the threshold of an era of fast, safe, comfortable and convenient transportation that might well be described as air-minded railroading."

In the design patents, Stout, plus Pullman and EMC people from Chicago were listed: Everett E. Adams,

Martin P. Blomberg, and William H. Mussey. The patents were assigned to Pullman.

Biographic sketches have, at most, a sentence about this railroad work. Stout is widely recognized for his automotive and aviation accomplishments. In 1919 he started Stout Engineering and in 1932 built the prototype Stout Scarab car. In 1934 he founded Stout Motor Car Company, which built nine beetlelike Scarabs featuring an all-aluminum tubular airframe and an engine compartment in the rear. The automotive successes led to an aviation career. He founded the Stout Metal Airplane Company in 1922 to build commercial metal planes. In 1924 Ford Motor Company purchased his company; he continued as vice president and general manager until 1930. Stout inaugurated Stout Air Services in 1925—the first scheduled airline in the United States, sold to United Airlines in 1929.

Stout listed many more accomplishments and maintained a sense of humor established early in his career when he contributed to the *Minneapolis Tribune* under the pen name Jack Knieff.

Union Pacific's first three Pullman-built streamliners shared similar styling and construction attributed to the work of William B. Stout and Martin Blomberg. UP's M-10002 was initially assigned as the *City of Los Angeles. Solomon collection*

The futuristic stainless-steel streamlining of Burlington's original Budd *Zephyr* inspired this fantasy train pictured racing past California orange groves. *Solomon collection*

Nevertheless it was still a remarkable achievement. When the sleek new machine left Pullman on February 12, 1934, it had required less than nine months to engineer and build. The M-10000 was just over 204 feet long and featured a wormlike shape unlike anything else on the continent. Its exterior was painted elegant shades of golden brown and canary yellow that was separated by thin red striping designed to accentuate the curves of the train and its sleek streamlined design. Inside, the train was decorated in shades of blue, with the ceiling nearly white and darker hues below the windows. To emphasize the train's construction, bands of polished aluminum were left exposed between various shades of blue, while seats were aluminum trimmed. Windows were shaded by Venetian blinds. In addition to an electric, forward-facing, fog-piercing headlight, the M-10000 featured a bright light that shined skyward to make the train more visible at night.

Burlington's *Zephyr*

On April 18, 1934, less than two months after Union Pacific's *Streamliner*, Burlington's revolutionary *Zephyr* made its public debut. On the surface this train appeared completely different. It took streamlined style in a completely different direction. But like the M-10000, its inspiration originated with McKeen, albeit via a different path. And, while the styling was different, both trains used EMC internal combustion engines and featured the same basic format: a unidirectional, three-piece articulated lightweight consist with a single power car upfront.

The *Zephyr* set important technological precedents. For propulsion, it was the first train powered by the Winton 201 diesel engine, which made it America's first diesel-powered streamliner—a bit of trivia that might have been less important if the diesel had not ultimately vanquished steam. From a streamlined perspective it was significant as well. The body was the work of Philadelphia-based Edward G. Budd Company (named for its founder, introduced in Chapter 1) and was constructed from shot-welded stainless steel using Budd's proprietary welding technique developed for automobile construction. Where

Burlington
Zephyr

1ST Streamline train in America
established in regular service

EAST and SOUTH	Lv Lincoln	7:30 am
	Ar Omaha	8:25 am
	Lv Omaha	9:00 am
	Lv Council Bluffs	9:10 am
	Lv St. Joseph	11:35 am
	Ar Kansas City	1:00 pm
NORTH and WEST	Lv Kansas City	2:30 pm
	Lv St. Joseph	3:55 pm
	Ar Council Bluffs	6:12 pm
	Ar Omaha	6:30 pm
	Lv Omaha	7:00 pm
	Ar Lincoln	7:55 pm

THE MOST ILLUSTRIOUS RAILROAD TRAIN IN THE WORLD

Built of stainless steel—Electric shot welded—Rides on articulated trucks. Powered by an eight-cylinder, two-cycle, 660 horse-power, oil-burning Diesel engine. Runs on roller-bearings—Air-conditioned—Equipped for radio reception.

Burlington's *Zephyr* was completed in April 1934 and was America's first high-speed, lightweight diesel-powered streamlined train. By contrast, Pullman's M-10000 was powered by a spark plug distillate-fueled engine. *Solomon collection*

Left: One of Burlington's early *Zephyr*s was photographed at Keokuk, Iowa, on June 12, 1940. *Paul Stringham, Jay Williams collection*

Below: Burlington introduced a pair of diesel-powered Budd shovelnose stainless-steel articulated streamlined trains in daily service on April 15, 1935, as the Chicago–Twin Cities *Twin Cities Zephyrs*. Burlington's second *Zephyr* set was a near copy of the 1934 original; it is pictured at St. Paul, Minnesota, in *Twin Cities Zephyrs* service in the mid-1930s. *Robert Graham, Jay Williams collection*

Pullman's *Railplane* and *Streamliner* forged new ground in their use of structural aluminum, *Zephyr* demonstrated the ability to use welded-steel construction that historically had been thought of as too weak for railroad vehicles.

Stylistically, *Zephyr*'s steeply pitched "shovel" nose seemed to resemble the polished helmet on a medieval suit of armor. This sent a significant psychological message demonstrating that the train was capable and strong. It was more than just a fancy railcar. Where UP's streamliner had featured a windowless rounded tail, the *Zephyr*'s tail car contained a lounge with large rear windows that allowed passengers to gaze back on the tracks. Like *Streamliner*, Burlington's Budd-built *Zephyr* made a public tour of the United States before entering revenue service.

Junior Knows It's an ELECTRIC Train

AND Junior's right. Electrons drive the wheels. These streamlined trains are *electric* trains—just as completely electric as though their power came from a third rail or an overhead wire. The husky electric motors that turn the wheels get their power from an electric generator driven by a diesel engine—a complete electric power plant right on the train.

It's electric drive that makes these trains glide along so smoothly and quietly, accelerate so rapidly, yet effortlessly. And

it's electricity that gives you adequate light for reading, conditioned air for comfort, and dozens of other conveniences found on these trains.

General Electric engineers have played a leading part in streamlined-train development—just as in all other forms of electric transportation. For more than 40 years these engineers have pioneered in building electric locomotives, and have brought you safer, faster, more comfortable transportation.

G-E research and engineering have saved the public from ten to one hundred dollars for every dollar they have earned for General Electric

GENERAL ⓖⓔ ELECTRIC

LISTEN TO THE G-E RADIO PROGRAM, MONDAYS, 9:30 P.M., E.S.T., NBC RED NETWORK

JANUARY 8, 1938

Boston & Maine's Budd-built streamliner No. 6000 appeared in this General Electric advertisement in 1938. This was a near duplicate of Burlington's original *Zephyr* and originally was assigned the name *Flying Yankee* for service between Boston, Portland, and Bangor, Maine. *Solomon collection*

ALBERT G. DEAN

by John Gruber

Albert G. Dean (1909–2002), an aeronautical engineer, designed the *Pioneer* and later *Zephyr* trains for the Budd Company, received his bachelor's degree from MIT in 1931 and did postgraduate work in metallurgy and aerodynamics. He went to work for Budd right after graduation. The training allowed him to design the aerodynamic exterior shape of the *Zephyr* to cut through the air for better top speed and fuel economy, and to design the stainless-steel structural shape of each car for minimum weight and maximum strength. He and Professor Shatswell Ober of MIT tested models in wind tunnels.

Two architectural firms created the cars' interiors. Winton built the diesel engine. American Flyer and Lionel immediately issued toy *Zephyrs*, capitalizing on the train's instant public success. The original 1934 *Pioneer Zephyr* is on permanent display at Chicago's Museum of Science and Industry, and the American Society of Mechanical Engineers designated it a landmark in 1980.

Dean was promoted to chief engineer of Budd's Railway Division in 1958 and was directly involved in every railcar Budd built during the life of the company, including the *Metroliner*, which served between New York City and Washington, DC, beginning in 1969. He was the sole or co-inventor of more than 115 US and foreign patents; these formed the core of Budd's foreign business. He traveled extensively in Europe and Japan to see the latest high-speed train technology and to recommend the best train designs for countries without extensive rail technology. Dean retired in 1969.

He was always enthusiastic about his work, according to a son, Clark Dean, but enjoyed camping, mountain climbing, and canoeing. He had a sense of humor about his problem-solving road trips. Summoned to Brazil because of rust stains, he got out a pencil eraser and easily rubbed the stains off the car. "It's disk brake dust that landed on the car surface while the cars were wet," he said. "Wash your cars."

Zephyr's design was the product of engineering genius, Edward Budd. Like Fetters, Budd had been involved in work on McKeen's railcars (see Chapter 1). A prolific innovator, in the 1920s Budd was interested in steel alloys and refined his "shot-welding" process to inexpensively weld stainless steels that were previously difficult to incorporate in manufactured products. Budd's earlier work with McKeen led him to revisit the subject in the 1930s when the Budd Company built a variety of innovative experimental lightweight railcars. Although commercial failures, these prototypes paved the way for his development work on Burlington's *Zephyr*. The unusual train name was derived from an ancient Greek god of wind called Zephyrus, and is believed to have been the inspiration of Burlington's leader, Ralph Budd (coincidentally, a distant relative of Edward G. Budd).

Budd employees A. G. Dean and E. J. W. Ragsdale executed important details of *Zephyr*'s structural design work.

Zephyr's influence not only redefined Budd's business in the midst of the Depression (enabling the company to become one of the leading passenger railcar manufacturers), but also propelled EMC into the business of diesel locomotive production. As a result of the success of these formative streamlined trains Budd, Pullman, and General Motors emerged as leading drivers of the streamlined era. However, what began as a means for applying aerodynamic design to railway vehicles rapidly evolved into a business model of commercial lightweight trains and diesel-electric motive power. Within a decade, "streamlined" had changed its meaning from "aerodynamic" to a blanket term inferring modern sleek styles, regardless of its true wind-resistant form.

In 1995, Burlington's *Pioneer Zephyr* underwent an extensive cosmetic restoration at Milwaukee's Northern Railcar. The intent was to return this significant train to its 1934 appearance for indoor display at the Museum of Science and Industry in Chicago. *Brian Solomon*

CHAPTER 3

THE FUSION OF SPEED AND STYLE

n the mid-1930s the streamlined train was born. Yet as quickly as streamlining attained popularity, it underwent a swift and unexpected transformation. In its early incarnation, streamlined trains represented an ideal and a distinct departure from conventional practice. They were highly refined, high-performance machines that blended the latest technologies and pushed the envelope of speed and service. Every effort was made to reduce weight and minimize wind resistance to make the most of modest internal combustion propulsion. The *Streamliner*, *Zephyr*, and their kin awed the industry and the public and changed the perception of the passenger train. They established new standards for construction and set a series of speed records.

In this incarnation, the American streamliner was typified by a super lightweight, low-center-of-gravity, articulated, and diesel-powered short consist. By 1936, the pendulum swung back; while streamlined styles and lightweight designs remained the driving features for an increasing number of new trains, the physical size and operational flexibility returned to more conventional formats typified by locomotive-hauled

continued on page 54

Opposite: In a thrilling display of steam, speed, and elegance, New York Central Dreyfuss-styled *20th Century Limited* races up the Hudson River Valley near Manitou, New York. In the distance the famed Bear Mountain Bridge spans the river. Dreyfuss streamlining was initially applied to ten brand new J-3a's in 1938 to coincide with introduction of the new *20th Century Limited. Edward L. May collection*

Budd's use of cold-rolled stainless steel combined great strength with corrosive-resistance and was easily welded using its patented shot-welding process. United States Steel Corporation provided Budd with the necessary grades of stainless steel to construct its trains. Among the stainless-steel beauties were Burlington's *Zephyrs*, the Reading *Crusader*, Seaboard Air Line's *Silver Meteor*, and Boston & Maine/Maine Central's *Zephyr* facsimile. *Solomon collection*

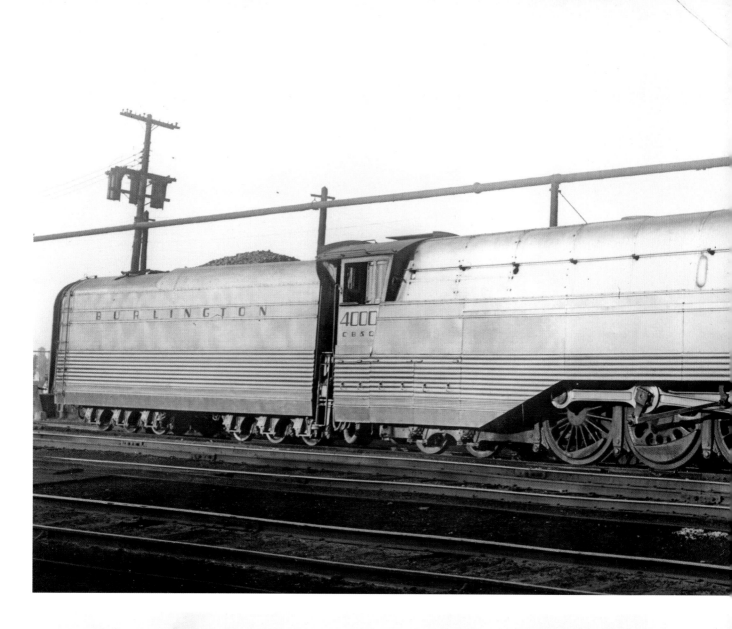

Left: Burlington applied Budd *Zephyr*-like stainless-steel shrouds to Hudson-type No. 4000, seen at Minneapolis, Minnesota, on October 1, 1938. Officially this engine carried the name *Æolus*, but it was commonly known as "Big Alice the Goon" after the popular comic book character of the period. Although its shrouds were removed, "Big Alice" survived scrapping and is displayed at La Crosse, Wisconsin. CB&Q also streamlined Hudson 4001 in a similar manner. *Jay Williams collection.*

Opposite below: Round-end observation cars were a feature of many streamlined trains. This Budd stainless-steel Buffet-Lounge-Observation was built for Atlantic Coast Line in 1939. It is pictured at Louisville, Kentucky, in 1942 on the back of the *Southwind*, a Chicago–Florida streamliner jointly operated every third day by ACL, Central of Georgia, Louisville & Nashville and Pennsylvania Railroad. *H. R. Blackburn, Jay Williams collection*

Below: A streamlined train and lower quadrant semaphores make for technological contrasts in this color-tinted postcard. Union Pacific's Pullman-built M-10006 *City of Denver* passes block signals on double track while racing across the plains. *Postcard, Solomon collection*

Overleaf: One of four Chesapeake & Ohio streamlined Hudsons passes Potomac Yard in Alexandria, Virginia, at the lead of No. 6, the *George Washington*, on August 8, 1947. *Bruce Fales, Jay Williams collection*

1110—Union Pacific Streamline Train. Overnight Service to the Rockies from the Mississippi

6A480

Rock Island was one of the earliest customers for Budd's full-size streamlined passenger cars. Observation car *Nebraska* was among the cars ordered for its *Rocket* streamliners of 1937. It was photographed on a *Rocket* set at 47th Street in Chicago on July 17, 1958. *Richard Jay Solomon*

Reading Company's unique *Crusader* streamliner included Budd-applied stainless-steel sheathing designed by John W. Patton for an older 4-6-2 Pacific locomotive. The sheathing was patented in 1941. Key to its design was the ability to run a round-end observation car flush with the locomotive tender to obviate the need to turn the train that ran with observation cars at both ends of the Budd-built stainless-steel consist. *1946 Reading Company timetable, Solomon collection*

continued from page 49
consists of streamlined, lightweight passenger cars with conventional nonarticulated couplings.

Electro-Motive's Transformation

Coincident with this evolution was Electro-Motive's rapid transformation from an engineering company to a full-scale locomotive manufacturer under the wing of automotive giant General Motors. While utilitarian switcher models dominated Electro-Motive's early diesel-electric locomotive production, by the late 1930s its streamlined passenger locomotives were among the most prominent diesels in America. Their streamlined styling and propulsion were a direct outgrowth of the early streamlined trains. Success in this market ultimately enabled Electro-Motive to become

MARTIN BLOMBERG

by Brian Solomon

The stylistic design evolution which dominated the steam to diesel transition years, from Pullman's early Winton Engine–powered articulated trains to Electro-Motive's E- and F-unit diesel locomotives, was the work of Martin Blomberg, one of the greatest unsung figures of the early streamlined era.

Blomberg was born in Sweden in 1888 and immigrated to North America before World War I, first to Canada, then the United States. Blomberg went to work for Pullman-Standard in 1925 where he was involved with carbody and wheel-set (truck) design. Later, he was closely involved with structural design for Pullman's early articulated trains, notably the streamlined trains for Union Pacific. Patents for the M-10000 and similar trains carry his name as well as Pullman's design consultant William B. Stout, plus Everett Adams (Union Pacific's engineering chief) and others. Stout is credited for the M-10000s aerodynamic shape, but the train's structural design was largely Blomberg's work. Patents credited to Stout, Blomberg, and Adams were all part of a unified effort for Pullman.

During 1935, Electro-Motive geared up to begin its own locomotive manufacturing as Pullman's role retreated to that of a passenger car manufacturer. Blomberg's work for Pullman was appreciated by his Electro-Motive counterparts. So in mid-1935 he resigned from Pullman to accept a position under Dick Dilworth at Electro-Motive. Over the next fourteen years his work helped shape Electro-Motive diesels during one of its most prolific periods. Best known of his contributions was his engineering for Electo-Motive's A1A and B-style trucks (wheel-sets) that carried his name. However, Blomberg's structural work also played a key role in the company's famous E- and F-units.

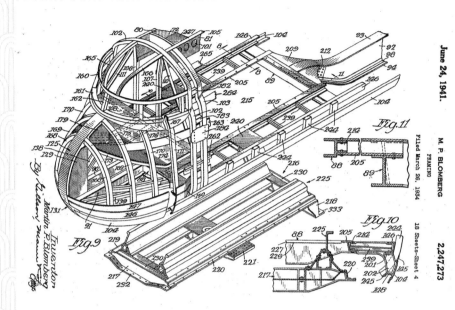

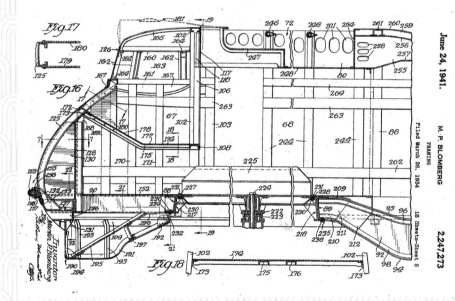

In his patent, Blomberg highlighted the principle objects of his innovation, including: the "desire to reduce weight without sacrificing strength; to adapt the framing to body shapes consistent with correct principle of aerodynamics; to provide the necessary strength for resisting front, side and rear impacts without unduly increasing the total weight of the car." This patent drawing reflects the shape used for Union Pacific's M-10000 power car. *United States Patent No. 2,247,273, June 24, 1941*

In 1938, New York Central hired Henry Dreyfuss, one of the most respected industrial designers of the prewar period, to restyle its flagship *20th Century Limited*. Dreyfuss dressed J-3a Hudsons in elegant shrouds and drafted the paint scheme and interiors. His vision of modernity complemented and contrasted with Raymond Loewy's designs for Central's chief competitor, Pennsylvania Railroad. Central's 1938 *20th Century Limited* and PRR's new *Broadway Limited* were debuted simultaneously as competing New York–Chicago luxury trains. *Robert A. Buck collection*

America's leading locomotive manufacturer. After World War II, most North American railroads bought diesels as fast as they could, which completely displaced steam power by 1960.

Transitional Electro-Motive Streamliners

The popularity of the early streamliners immediately encouraged more trains. Both Burlington and Union Pacific built families of streamlined trains based on the respective designs debuted by the *Zephyr* and *Streamliner*. Streamlining was contagious, and railroads placed orders with Budd, Pullman, and other manufacturers for modern lightweight, streamlined

New York Central's new streamlined *Empire State Express* made its debut with a special press run on December 7, 1941. Unfortunately for Central, its flashy press campaign was lost as this day will forever be remembered in the words of United States president, Franklin D. Roosevelt, as "a date which will live in infamy." World War II had profound effects on American railroading. In 1946, after hostilities had concluded, New York Central was still content to display its *Empire State Express* on the cover of its public timetable. *Solomon collection*

trains with Electro-Motive diesel propulsion. (Strictly speaking, it was General Motors' Winton Diesel Corp that provided engines in the early days, but with the establishment of Electro-Motive as a locomotive manufacturer, Winton Diesel's name was de-emphasized.)

Union Pacific's initial M-10000 didn't have carrying capacity for anything more than a relatively short run, and after its publicity tours it entered service on January 31, 1935, as the relatively obscure *City of Salina* train. Even before UP's concept train hit the rails, the railroad had ordered another train, the M-10001, featuring a similar design but with a nine-car consist and a more powerful engine (this time a diesel) that was intended for transcontinental service. It made a lightning-fast run from Los Angeles to Chicago, exceeding all speed records, before entering Chicago–Portland service as the *City of Portland* on June 6, 1935. UP ordered

a third Pullman train, M-10002, with an eleven-car consist powered by dual Winton diesels, together rated at 2,100 horsepower. This entered *City of Los Angeles* service (Chicago–Los Angeles) on May 15, 1936, in direct competition with Santa Fe's new diesel-powered *Super Chief*, which began just three days earlier.

After M-10002, the shape of Union Pacific's Pullman power cars evolved. Power cars for M-10003 through M-10006 featured automotive styling with a raised cab profile and broad grille. Power car M-10004 was powered by dual 1,200-horsepower Winton-diesels that led a twelve-car luxury train built for weekly service as the *City of San Francisco*. West of Ogden, Utah, this train used Southern Pacific's line over Donner Pass to reach Oakland, California, across San Francisco Bay from its namesake.

continued on page 60

A westbound *Rocket* pauses for passengers at Englewood, Illinois, on July 13, 1940. The locomotive, Electro-Motive E6A 628 is only a month old at the time, bought to supplement Rock Island's unique fleet of Electro-Motive TAs built in 1937. The E6A was the most widely built prewar E-unit model with 120 units built, and the last to feature the steeply pitched nose. Postwar E-units used the more conservative "bulldog nose" developed in 1939 for the FT. *Robert A. Buck collection*

15861. Streamliner, "City of Los Angeles" Union Pacific System

This 1930s postcard view purports to depict the M-10002 that worked as the *City of Los Angeles*. However, in fact it shows the shorter consist of the M-10001 that was assigned to the *City of Portland*. *Solomon collection*

In a vision of modern railroading, the then nearly new Burlington *Zephyr* 9903 named *Injun Joe* pauses for a station stop at Hannibal, Missouri, on April 12, 1936. The shovelnose trains remained a common sight on Burlington for decades. *Robert A. Buck collection*

Boston & Maine and Maine Central's Budd-built articulated train initially worked as the *Flying Yankee* but was known colloquially as the "Silver Fish." This hand-tinted postcard pictures it arriving on its scheduled run at Orchard Beach, Maine. *Solomon collection*

The original *City of San Francisco* made its debut in May 1936 using this Pullman-built lightweight train. It is seen on Southern Pacific crossing the Great Salt Lake in Utah. In December 1937, Union Pacific introduced its all-new fourteen-car *City of San Francisco* hauled by an A-B-B Electro-Motive E2 set. *Solomon collection*

continued from page 57

An article in January 10, 1936, *Diesel Railway Traction* indicates that M-10004 was an important transitional train in UP's fleet built in accordance with A. H. Fetters input. *City of San Francisco*'s passenger cars shared common characteristics and construction with the earlier trains (although not completely articulated), though the power cars were different, setting new precedents for diesel locomotive–hauled trains. Notably, they were not articulated and rode on more conventionally powered wheel-sets. Also the bodies were made from riveted Cor-Ten steel with straight sides, rather than tubular aluminium construction, and were taller and wider than the earlier power cars. For these later streamliners UP used locomotive-hauled consists, although it retained elements of the early lightweight designs, including aluminum construction. Later power cars (M-10003 to M-10006) were 15½ inches taller than M-10000. The M-10005 and M-10006 were assigned to the daily *City of Denver* with twelve car-sets.

continued on page 64

Above: Union Pacific's M-10003 to M-10006 power cars were built by Pullman and powered by Winton diesels. The car bodies were made from riveted Cor-Ten steel, while styling took its cues from automotive design and hinted at shapes to come for Electro-Motive's early E-units. In the mid-1930s, a pair of the distinctive streamlined sets for *City of Denver* and *City of Los Angeles* were seen at C&NW's Chicago coach yards. *Robert A. Buck collection*

Opposite: In 1937, Union Pacific ordered two fourteen-car streamlined Pullman trains each hauled by sets of specially built three-unit Electro-Motive E2 diesels. The first was assigned to *City of Los Angeles* and the second to *City of San Francisco*. The *City of Los Angeles* is pictured in this 1930s Union Pacific advertisement. The two sets of A-B-B E2s were the only example of that model built, and they shared technical characteristics with Baltimore & Ohio's EA/EBs and Santa Fe's E1A/E1Bs. *Solomon collection*

Overleaf: Illinois Central's *Green Diamond* was brand-new when put on public display at 115th Street in Cottage Grove, Chicago on March 20, 1936. After an extensive tour of Illinois Central's lines, the train entered service on the premier Chicago–St Louis run, where IC competed with three other carriers for passenger traffic. *J. Michael Gruber collection*

continued from page xx

Ahead of the Future

The keynote of American progress is individual enterprise and initiative. As a nation, we plan ahead—not only for tomorrow but for the day after tomorrow. Thinking "ahead of the future" resulted, for example, in the building of the fleet of America's first streamlined trains—the Union Pacific Streamliners.

Far-sighted planning and individual enterprise have played a tremendous part in the growth of America. In 1859, Abraham Lincoln foresaw the vital need for a transcontinental railroad that would unite the East with the West in peace and in war. Today, over the Strategic Middle Route of the Union Pacific Railroad speed hundreds of trainloads of troops, foods, and materials of war. Rail transportation makes it possible for America to carry on the fight for freedom.

* * *

Many thousands of Union Pacific employes are working—many thousands fighting—to keep alive the American tradition of equal opportunity for all; to insure a just reward in return for hard work, for enterprise and for faith in the nation's future.

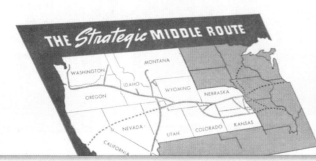

THE PROGRESSIVE

UNION PACIFIC RAILROAD

Color photographs of Illinois Central's original *Green Diamond* streamliner are rare. This was exposed on Kodachrome, the commercial transparency film that Kodak debuted in 1936 within months of the *Green Diamond* entering service. Although it shared similar structure with Pullman's earlier trains built for Union Pacific, period sources indicate that *Green Diamond* was made from riveted Cor-Ten steel, rather than aluminum. *J. Michael Gruber collection*

continued from page 60
Illinois Central *Green Diamond*

Related to Union Pacific's streamliners was Pullman's unique articulated train built for Illinois Central as its *Green Diamond*. Its name was an outgrowth of IC's emblematic heritage. IC, like other major coal-hauling railroads, had adopted the diamond for its herald. In the early years of the twentieth century, railroads competing for Chicago–St. Louis passenger traffic adopted colors for their premier passenger trains: Wabash chose blue, Alton a reddish maroon, and Illinois Central opted for green. IC's streamliner, adorned in two-tone green, was the latest incarnation of this image, and represented a deliberate effort to gain market share in the Chicago–St. Louis market.

Illinois Central and Union Pacific shared a common direction from the Harriman family, dating to E. H. Harriman's control in the late nineteenth century. In the 1930s, Harriman's son, W. Averell Harriman, was both president of Union Pacific and a board member of Illinois Central. Since both Harrimans were key figures in development of Union Pacific's advanced internal combustion trains, it stands to reason that IC benefited from this influence as well.

IC's five-car articulated train was powered by a 1,200-horsepower Winton diesel. Following the power car was a mail and baggage car, two chair car coaches, and a kitchen-lounge-observation. It is noteworthy as the only such streamliner bought by IC and the last fully articulated streamliner built by Pullman.

While its stylistic lineage originated with Pullman's *Railplane* and its obvious similarity to the early Union Pacific articulated trains, IC's *Green Diamond* was not made from aluminum. *Diesel Railway Traction* profiled the train in May 15, 1936, describing its tubular structure and noting that "all the main frame members of plate, rolled, and bar sections, and the panel plates are of Cor-Ten steel." At the time of delivery, *Railway Age* wrote that the train weighed 230 tons when empty, which was about half the weight of a conventional train.

Green Diamond enjoyed a public tour before entering revenue service in May 1936, running a daily 588-mile roundtrip. After World War II, the set was renamed and briefly reallocated to the New Orleans–Jackson, Mississippi, run. It was withdrawn in 1949, and scrapped about 1950.

continued on page 68

A chill in the air results in a wisp of condensation from the steam line on Burlington's Denver *Zephyr* at its Colorado terminus in February 1953. The stainless-steel Budd-built observation car was a classic feature of many Burlington streamlined trains. Here passengers could watch the rails recede behind them at speed in climate-controlled comfort. *Wallace A. Abbey, courtesy of the Center for Railroad Photography & Art, www.railphoto-art.org*

Overleaf: Preserved Burlington E5A 9911A and Atlantic Coast Line E3A 501 demonstrate characteristics of Electro-Motive's prewar E-units that featured a steeply pitched front end, elegant number boards, and subtle car body refinements. Notice the difference in the style of the headlights between the two locomotives. The *Zephyr*-like vents on the E5A are strictly styling and have no practical function. *Brian Solomon*

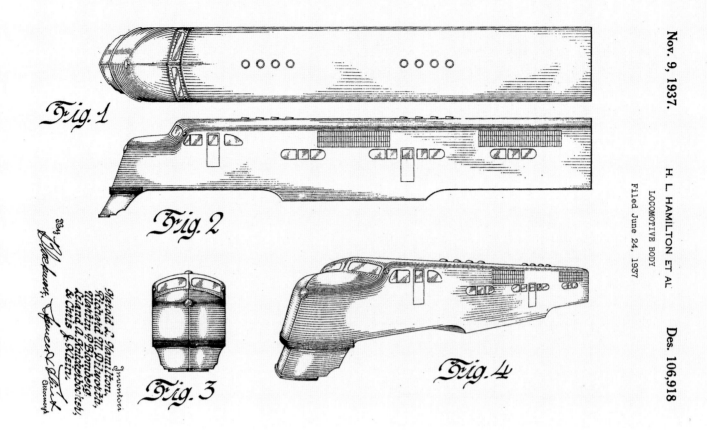

Nov. 9, 1937.

H. L. HAMILTON ET AL
LOCOMOTIVE BODY
Filed June 24, 1937

Des. 106,918

Electro-Motive's E-unit's distinctive car body was the culmination of several years of streamlined evolution that began with Pullman's *Railplane* of 1933. Electro-Motive's founder Harold L. Hamilton, its top engineer Richard M. Dilworth, former Pullman engineer Martin P. Blomberg, Leland A. Knickerbocker, and Chris J. Klein were listed on this 1937 design patent for the original E-unit locomotive body. *United States Design Patent No. 106,918, November 9, 1937*

---

continued from page 65

Zephyr Evolution

During the mid-1930s, Burlington's Budd-stainless-steel trains underwent a similar design evolution as UP's trains. Following successful public demonstrations of the original *Zephyr*, Burlington ordered more trains of the same essential design, but with four-car articulated consists. The original train was named *Pioneer Zephyr* and initially entered service on a low-profile midwestern run in late 1934. The nearly identical four trains were placed in service in daily high-speed Chicago–Twin Cities service as the *Twin Zephyrs* on April 21, 1935, and another trainset began service as the *Mark Twain Zephyr* a little more than six months later.

Burlington's short, fast consists were a hit with the riding public, and so the railroad needed longer trains to accommodate demand. Writing in August 13, 1938, *Railway Age*, Burlington's president Ralph Budd reviewed his railroad's recent history and articulated his policy changes that reflected the future of the American passenger train:

The underlying virtue of weight reduction is the avoidance of work, that is the saving in expenditure of energy, while the underlying virtue of the Diesel-electric locomotive is efficient performance . . . From an engineering standpoint the two constitute an ideal combination.

Electro-Motive Corporation placed a striking front cover advertisement in January 26, 1936, *Railway Age*:

Distinctive in their streamline design . . . outstanding in their beauty of appointments . . . remarkable in their smooth effortless operation over the rails . . . such are the attributes of the now famous *Twin Zephyrs*. But of far greater importance is their factor of power that has made possible a record of uninterrupted service . . . their Electro-Motive Diesel powerplants.

Like UP, Burlington moved away from fixed consists in favor of locomotive-hauled compact lightweight trains. Burlington further expanded its *Zephyr* family. It bought four passenger diesels from Electro-Motive in 1936 with shovelnose styling that were powered by pairs of Winton 900-horsepower diesels. These were among the first locomotives built by Electro-Motive at its new LaGrange, Illinois, factory and anticipated the format of E-unit models that soon followed.

Boston & Maine/Maine Central had been impressed by Burlington's original *Zephyr* and jointly had placed an order with Budd for a near duplicate. This was delivered in early 1935 and began service as the *Flying Yankee* on April 1. The train was a New England sensation running an aggressive daily roundtrip schedule connecting Boston's North Station with Portland and Bangor, Maine. In later years this train worked various named services, including the *Mountaineer* and *Cheshire*. The set survives, having been displayed at Edaville in southeastern Massachusetts for decades. It has been undergoing a prolonged restoration at Claremont, New Hampshire, and may eventually return to operation.

Electro-Motive's E-Units

Electro-Motive built boxcab experimentals in 1935, which established mechanical precedents for development of the company's stand-alone diesel-electric passenger locomotive. While the boxcabs were functional, Electro-Motive had recognized that streamlined style was the order of the day and set out to design an all-new passenger locomotive. Its engineers incorporated the best qualities of the early streamliners and boxcab locomotive designs while integrating a host of technological improvements. Dick Dilworth designed the new passenger locomotive to match performance characteristics of the best Hudson-type steam locomotives, a type considered as the most advanced steam locomotive of its time.

Major changes were made with the cab arrangement in order to give crews greater protection in the event of collision. The cab was elevated and set back from the front with a protective reinforced nose

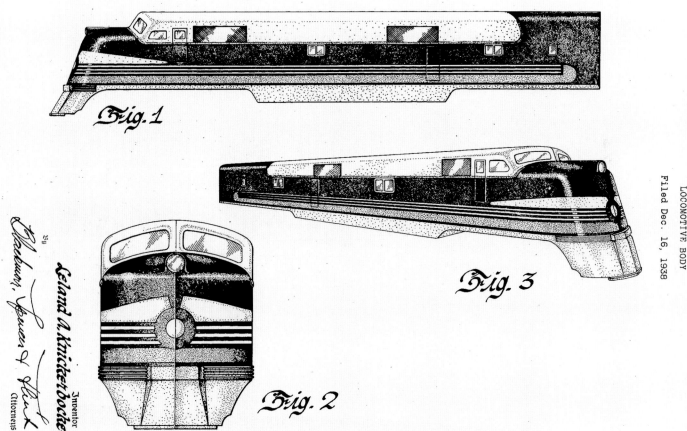

Feb. 28, 1939.　　L. A. KNICKERBOCKER　　Des. 113,563

LOCOMOTIVE BODY

Filed Dec. 16, 1938

Leland A. Knickerbocker
Inventor

Attorneys

General Motors designer Leland A. Knickerbocker is most famous for his design of Santa Fe's warbonnet paint scheme, but he was also instrumental in the early styling of Electro-Motive's E-unit. His design patent was filed in December 1938 and reflects the styling applied to model E4, built for Seaboard Air Line, a railroad that was among the earliest user of production-built road diesels. *United States Design Patent No. 113,563, February 28, 1939*

Lifeline OF TOMORROW

RISING magnificently to cope with every disaster and emergency for nearly a century, the American railroads have just re-verified the statement that they are "the lifeline of the nation." Manpower, equipment and multitudinous other problems were met and overcome.

Wartime restrictions curtailed improvements and construction, but not planning. And, that planning takes in trains, tracks, terminals — a gamut of seen and behind-the-scene factors. When welded with new materials, new and improved methods, trains that will far surpass anything previously offered — in luxury and style, comfort and service — will emerge from this planning. We of the Seaboard look forward with confidence to the day we enter this role.

Now that Peace reigns again; the saga of American heroes has been written, the Seaboard, together with the other railroads, will again demonstrate and win the approbation of the public as "the lifeline of the nation" . . . a lifeline that will aid us to better enjoy the better way of life promised for the better world of tomorrow.

Our original locomotive, imported from England in 1836. Since that early date, our parent companies and the present Seaboard system have been providing progressively finer service.

Streamlined visions sometimes varied from reality: this stylistic drawing from Seaboard Air Line's November 1945 public timetable depicts a fantastic future streamliner loosely patterned on SAL's prewar *Orange Blossom Special* that featured Electro-Motive E4 diesel with Budd-built stainless-steel cars. *Solomon collection*

City of San Francisco was jointly run by Chicago & North Western, Union Pacific, and Southern Pacific between Chicago and Oakland, California. In 1937 the train was re-equipped with a full-sized fourteen-car lightweight consist hauled by a three-unit set of specially built Electro-Motive E2 diesels. It is seen arriving at C&NW Terminal in Chicago, circa 1939. The streamlined train contrasts with the antique Hall "banjo" signal on the bridge to the right of the train. Saboteurs in the Nevada desert tragically derailed this train on August 28, 1939. *Robert A. Buck collection*

---

designed to deflect objects while providing forward visibility and shielding the view of tracks passing below. The cab and rounded nose modifications were a concurrent adoption of a framed body structure that served as an integral support structure rather than just an external covering. B&O, Santa Fe, and Union Pacific bought early custom-styled E-units. Mass-produced E-units began with model E3 in March 1939.

Baltimore & Ohio

In 1935 Baltimore & Ohio introduced a modern, lightweight train that was widely publicized as one of the most innovative of the era. Yet, because it was neither diesel-powered nor fully streamlined, this train was soon forgotten despite the fact that the cars

Functionally, the E5 was the same as E3, E4, and E6 models but featured stainless-steel styling to match Budd-built passenger cars and closely resembled the early *Zephyr* power cars. The model was built from February 1940 to June 1941, and consisted of eleven cab units and five boosters. *Brian Solomon*

NORTH WESTERN'S FAMOUS STREAMLINER "400" OPERATES DAILY BETWEEN CHICAGO AND ST. PAUL-MINNEAPOLIS VIA MILWAUKEE

Above: In January 1935, C&NW was first to improve its Chicago–Twin Cities services with its new, tightly scheduled, traditionally steam-hauled *Twin Cities 400*. This traveled 409 miles in seven hours—roughly 400 miles in 400 minutes—thus the train's name. C&NW's *400*-brand was used as its new theme for passenger services that ultimately adopted streamlined styles. Diesels were first assigned to the *Twin Cities 400*s in 1939. *Color postcard, Solomon collection*

Below: Chicago, Burlington & Quincy 9911-A is the only surviving Electro-Motive E5A and is preserved in operating condition at the Illinois Railway Museum at Union. *Brian Solomon*

survived longer in service than other, better known pioneer streamliners.

May 4, 1935, *Railway Age* focused on B&O's lightweight trains: a pair built by ACF at St. Charles, Missouri, for service between Chicago and St. Louis on the Alton Route as the *Abraham Lincoln* and *Ann Rutledge*. (B&O acquired the Chicago & Alton in the 1920s, renamed it the Alton, and operated it until 1943 before selling the line to GM&O.) ACF's two eight-car trainsets used different materials: one was made from United States Steel's Cor-Ten steel alloys; the other had a body constructed from aluminum alloys with a steel underframe. Both used essentially the same structure with nominal differences to account for the characteristics of the different metals. Each was 557 feet, 10 inches long, with coach seating capacity for 283 passengers and an additional 42 nonrevenue seats in the diner. Although the cars used a low profile—a roofline 16 inches lower than a conventional B&O heavyweight car—in most other respects the cars were full-sized to give passengers ample space and comfort inside.

Weight reduction was the primary emphasis of the design, but *Railway Age* noted that the cars incorporated notable wind-resistant features: the roofs were

Alco brought out its road diesel in late 1939 that used the equipment pattern established by Electro-Motive's E-unit, but with a distinctive streamlined Kuhler-styled car body. Its futuristic design contrasted with Electro-Motive's automobile-like styling. Rock Island bought the prototype, specification number DL-103, followed by similar production units for service on its *Rockets* streamliners but later assigned to less prestigious runs. This DL-107 was pictured at Fort Worth, Texas, on October 5, 1948. *Haney photo, Jay Williams collection*

rounded with minimal protrusions, sides were skirted, windows were flush, and vestibule steps folded into the body of the car, while the tail cars featured a rounded, teardrop profile. An ACF advertisement pointed out that "an interesting innovation is the closure between cars, designed to flex with the train movement. This arrangement continues the smooth surface of the perimeter line of the cars giving to the entire train the appearance of a single-unit and materially reducing air-drag." So the trains really were streamlined, except for the locomotives. As built, the trains were painted in a dark blue with gray roofs and trucks, with lettering in classy gold leaf.

In 1934, Baltimore & Ohio built two very unusual steam locomotives for fast lightweight service. B&O had been experimenting with innovative steam design under the direction of motive power chief George Emerson; these lightweight engines featured high-pressure Emerson water-tube fireboxes and fire-tube boiler sheets. Engine 1, *Lady Baltimore* Class J-1, used the rare 4-4-4 wheel arrangement, while engine 2, *Lord Baltimore* Class V-2, was a 4-6-4 Hudson type. Both shared similar styling, including a British-style firebox door. Among its duties, *Lady Baltimore* worked lightweight trains in *Royal Blue* service between Jersey City and Washington, before being replaced by an early Electro-Motive boxcab diesel. In the book *B&O Power*, published in 1964, Lawrence W. Sagle and Alvin F. Staufer offer a story that *Lady Baltimore* was intended as a streamlined engine, and in fact was provisionally shrouded, but when the railroad's president, strong-willed "Uncle Dan" Willard, saw the locomotive, he demanded that the shrouds be removed. If the account is accurate, it hints that this B&O engine was actually the first North American locomotive built as a streamliner.

B&O revisited streamlined steam in 1937 when it hired industrial designer Otto Kuhler to style rebuilt

On August 6, 1939, a Baltimore & Ohio B&O EA/EB set leads train 26, *The Columbian* (Washington DC to Chicago) at Muirkirk, Maryland. Notice the mix of streamlined and conventional equipment. B&O was the first to buy Electro-Motive E-units, and its six A- and six B-units represented the entire production run for the model EA. On the E-unit, Electro-Motive designers relocated car body vents to the sides of the locomotive to improve air circulation. *Bruce Fales, Jay Williams collection*

standard-weight cars and a Presidential P-7 4-6-2 Pacific 5304. The locomotive received impressive shrouds with a bulletlike front end. It was painted blue and renamed from *President Monroe* to *Royal Blue* for service on the train of the same name. Locomotive 5304's initial streamlined experience was short-lived. In 1940, B&O removed the shrouds and returned the engine to regular passenger service. However, it was restreamlined in 1946, along with three other Presidential Pacifics, at B&O's Mt. Clare Shops for

service on the *Cincinnatian*. For this design, B&O hired Olive Dennis (see sidebar on page 140).

B&O was also a streamlined diesel pioneer. In 1935 it bought a lone 1,800-horsepower boxcab from Electro-Motive (which was later given a semi-streamlined treatment, and worked lightweight trains, including the *Royal Blue*). This acquisition paved the way for B&O to order the first fully streamlined, stand-alone passenger locomotives (as distinguished from earlier diesel power cars that were semi-permanently coupled to trainsets),

"20TH CENTURY LIMITED"

The ability of streamlined trains to create traffic is demonstrated by this splendid new "Twentieth Century" of the New York Central. During the period from June 15 to November 15, 1938, it carried 27,568 passengers from New York to Chicago—an increase of 38% over the number carried during the same period before the train was streamlined. The cars built by Pullman Standard Car Manufacturing Company, are the last word in comfort and convenience. In their construction U·S·S COR-TEN and U·S·S MAN-TEN play a vital part in saving about 1/3 the weight of conventional cars.

"GREEN DIAMOND"

Placed in service on the Illinois Central May 17, 1936, this 5-car fully articulated streamliner makes the 588-mile round-trip between Chicago and St. Louis daily at an average speed of 60 m.p.h. Effective air conditioning, smooth riding qualities at high speed, and its fast schedule recommend it to the traveling public. In this train, built by Pullman, U·S·S COR-TEN sheets and plates, riveted and welded, replace the usual rolled sections of mild steel make it possible to reduce weight to about 50% of conventional trains used for same service.

"ANN RUTLEDGE"

This beautifully styled and completely appointed 8-car streamlined COR-TEN train, of the Baltimore and Ohio-Alton, was built by the American Car and Foundry Company. It operates the 282 miles between Chicago and St. Louis—a round trip daily—at an average speed of 56 m.p.h. Train complete weighs approximately 284 tons less, 40% less, than conventional construction. Indicative of the patronage this train has received is the fact that for the seven months ending June 30th, 1938, its total revenue was $309,123   net revenue $181,763 or 58.8%.

This late-1930s United States Steel Corporation advertisement shows four trains made from Cor-Ten Steel, a lightweight, rust-resistant, chromium-copper-silicon steel alloy. From top to bottom are New York Central's 1938 *20th Century Limited*, Illinois Central's *Green Diamond*, Baltimore & Ohio's *Ann Rutledge*, and one of Gulf, Mobile & Northern's *Rebels*. The ad's train placement is prescient: by 1945, both of the bottom two trains would be operated by the newly formed Gulf, Mobile & Ohio. *Solomon collection*

Baltimore & Ohio's one-of-kind lightweight Hudson *Lord Baltimore* departs Washington, DC, with the *Royal Blue* at 4:20 p.m. on February 9, 1936. B&O was a lightweight pioneer and both the locomotive and passengers cars were built to advanced designs. *Bruce Fales, Jay Williams collection*

Left: Baltimore & Ohio's December 12, 1943, public timetable features one of its Electro-Motive EA diesels to promote its streamlined trains. *Baltimore & Ohio timetable, Solomon collection*

ISSUED DECEMBER 12, 1943.

B&O
SCHEDULES
of Thru
MAIN LINE
TRAINS

BALTIMORE & OHIO R.R
ROUTE OF THE DIESEL-ELECTRIC POWER STREAMLINERS

models EA/EB, Electro-Motive's first successful E-units. B&O's model EA No. 51, built in May 1937, deemed first of its kind, has been preserved at the Baltimore & Ohio Railroad Museum in Baltimore.

Santa Fe Streamliners

Santa Fe took a deliberate, yet cautious approach toward its adoption of streamlined trains. It was impressed by the potential as a means to reinvigorate passenger train traffic, but instead of ordering a package deal like Burlington or Union Pacific, it first sampled elements of the new technologies independently. The articulated, pocket-sized, diesel-streamliner was like a custom-designed, tailor-made suit; fantastic to

Along Your Way

Facts about stations and scenes on the Santa Fe

A Santa Fe brochure displays its classic E1-hauled *Super Chief*. Santa Fe's E1A/E1B diesels were the first application of the warbonnet paint scheme designed by Electro-Motive artist Leland A. Knickerbocker. This distinctive red, yellow, black, and silver scheme became emblematic of the modern Santa Fe, and was one of the most recognized North America railway paint schemes. *Solomon collection*

One of Santa Fe's semi-streamlined Electro-Motive boxcabs leads the *Super Chief* at Galesburg, Illinois, on August 8, 1937. *R. C. Bell, Jay Williams collection*

impress at an evening event, but impractical as day-to-day apparel. Santa Fe sampled its new clothing from a variety of purveyors and ultimately assembled a whole new versatile wardrobe that was good for all occasions. By so doing, Santa Fe set the fashion for the whole industry.

The railroad was no stranger to self-propelled internal combustion trains; like many railroads of the period, it had fleets of gas-electrics for passenger services on branch lines. It was familiar with Electro-Motive railcars, and had been one of the company's best customers. Santa Fe had much to gain by internal combustion innovation since it had many long runs, and served some of the driest areas of the country where procuring clean water suitable for locomotive boilers proved to be complex and costly. In 1935,

Santa Fe began dieselization with acquisition of an Alco 660-horsepower high-hood switcher for service in Chicago. More significantly, in October 1935 it purchased a pair of Electro-Motive's experimental diesel-electric boxcabs, similar to the one bought by B&O, for use on a new transcontinental express passenger service called the *Super Chief*.

The diesel enabled Santa Fe to operate a faster schedule than possible with its existing steam power. *Railway Age* in October 1935 noted that "if exhaustive tests prove successful," Santa Fe planned for regular diesel service. Despite their boxy design, the locomotives exhibited nominal external styling crafted by General Motors that included a distinctive paint scheme blending an array of colors, including cobalt and Sarasota blue, scarlet, and a shade of golden olive, on what was a dominantly black body.

A potential setback occurred a month or so after the boxcabs entered service, when on an L.A. run a fueling mishap resulted in a serious fire that badly damaged one of the locomotives. Undaunted, Santa Fe continued with its plans. Not only were the boxcabs repaired, but in 1937 it was among the first lines to receive Electro-Motive E-units.

Santa Fe wanted a lightweight passenger car design without being restricted to constraining articulated trainsets, which suffered from claustrophobic spaces and were incompatible with existing equipment. The company took its cues from Burlington and worked with the Budd Company in the design of full-sized, conventionally proportioned stainless-steel passenger cars that it could use as part of a consist of existing heavyweight cars. Budd delivered experimental coach No. 3070 to Santa Fe in early 1936. Although it was unique in its structural design, Santa Fe's stainless-steel prototype set a pattern for streamlined train construction adopted by railroads across the continent and around the world.

In designing 3070, Budd adopted an experimental design and departed from aspects of the *Zephyr*'s structure in an effort to simplify the fabrication process. In place of the side-panel truss frames, 3070 used large upright channels. While the car proved itself in service, this design was abandoned, and later cars returned to the Pratt-style side trusses.

Santa Fe took a pragmatic approach to speeding up long-distance schedules, largely accomplished by limiting stops en route and keeping station stops to just a few minutes, while maintaining quick over-the-road speeds. Diesels were used for this strategy, although Santa Fe was soon pushing the limits of modern steam power as well.

In November 1936, Santa Fe debuted its most famous train, the now legendary *Super Chief*. This *continued on page 82*

Overleaf: Santa Fe's only streamlined steam locomotive was a Baldwin Hudson 3460, a high-performance machine known as the "Blue Goose" because of its two-tone blue paint, and later as the "Mae West" for losing its skirting. Popular with model railroaders, Santa Fe 3460 has been replicated in the thousands. *Robert A. Buck collection*

Below: Harold Hamilton's design patent for the E1A body style displays the essential elements of Santa Fe's famous warbonnet livery. This scheme was adopted by Santa Fe and applied to many locomotive models, including those built by Electro-Motive's competitors, Alco and Fairbanks-Morse. *United States Design Patent, 106,920, Nov 9, 1937*

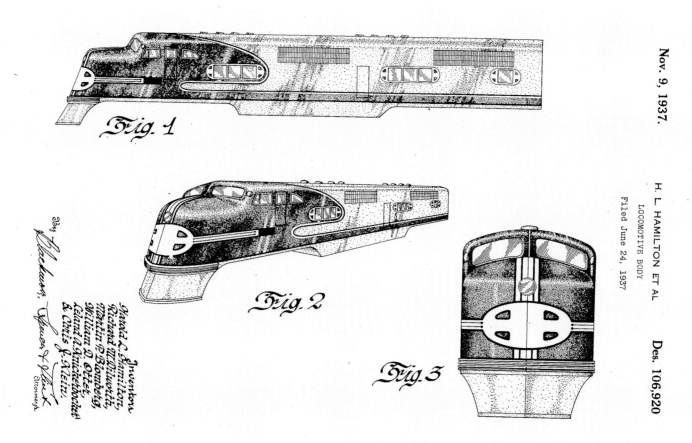

Nov. 9, 1937.

H. L. HAMILTON ET AL
LOCOMOTIVE BODY
Filed June 24, 1937

Des. 106,920

Fig. 1

Fig. 2

Fig. 3

One of Milwaukee Road's distinctive and so-called beaver tail parlor observations built by its Milwaukee shops for service on the very fast *Hiawatha*. *Milwaukee Road photo by Harvey Uecker, Jay Williams collection*

continued from page 79
began as a once weekly, extra-fare, first-class, super-fast Chicago–L.A. service. In its original configuration, it wasn't a streamliner, but a boxcab diesel-hauled train of deluxe heavyweight sleepers. The extra-special *Super Chief* sprinted from Chicago's Dearborn Station to Los Angeles in under forty hours.

The fully streamlined *Super Chief* followed a few months later, when on May 18, 1937, the nine-car sleek stainless-steel Budd-built train began once per week "sailing" from Chicago to Los Angles. Unlike earlier Budd streamliners, this was the first completely comprised of full-sized conventionally coupled cars, hauled by a locomotive. It was a landmark train. Not just because of its captivating style and flashy appearance, but it helped establish a new pattern for the American passenger train. From this point forward, heavyweight cars were out of fashion, and articulated lightweights remained anomalies to conventional practice.

Super Chief was designed as a first-class, extra-fare, sleeping car train, its specialized consist embraced comfort over capacity. It was intended to attract affluent passengers accustomed to luxury and specious accommodation. In *Railroads of Today*, S. Kip Farrington wrote that *Super Chief*'s equipment was "second to none." He elaborated, "Regardless of where you are aboard the *Super Chief* there is always a luxurious lounge compartment close by." Although awed by the train, he was less than taken by the route it took, which he found monotonous.

Super Chief was a rolling embodiment of stylized Native American art designed to key in on the traditional character of the southwestern route. For this train, and the fleet that followed, Santa Fe bought eleven E1A and E1B models from Electro-Motive that were among their first production passenger diesels. Each of these sleek streamlined locomotive units were powered by a pair of Winton diesel engines and painted in the classic warbonnet livery.

Super Chief's interior design was jointly contrived by Santa Fe's advertising manager Roger W. Birdseye, Philadelphia architect Paul F. Cret, and Chicago decorator Sterling B. McDonald. The train's rounded-end sleeper/observation *Navajo* offered the most impressive artistic interpretation. Its rear-facing lounge was equipped with swiveling seats mounted laterally along sides of the car. The car displayed *Navajo* themes throughout; its colors mimicked the southwestern landscape while the walls were decorated with examples of sand painting. Santa Fe prided itself in attention to detail. *Super Chief*'s Mimbreño-style dining car china was the design of Mary Colter, an avid student of southwestern art. Named for the Mimbres tribe of southwestern New Mexico, its patterns featured animal icons and shapes, and it was considered some of the finest china to serve the public aboard an American passenger train.

More Streamliners

The new streamlined *Super Chief* was an immediate hit with the more affluent traveling public and a roaring success for Santa Fe. The railroad was quick to build upon *Super Chief*, using this train as the pattern for a whole fleet of similarly styled trains. In the spring of 1938, it debuted a host of new trains, deemed by *Railway Age* as the largest fleet of modern, lightweight streamlined trains in the world. These became legends of American railroad travel.

In addition to the E-units fleets, Santa Fe simultaneously placed an order with Baldwin for state-of-the-art, high-speed 4-6-4 Hudson-type steam locomotives, numbered in the 3460-series and delivered in 1937. They were designed to rival diesel performance on the long run between Chicago and La Junta, Colorado, and had some of the tallest driving wheels of any modern American steam locomotive, measuring 7 feet high. In a special publicity run on December 9, 1937, Santa Fe 3461 set the world record for the longest continuous steam run, from Los Angeles all the way to Chicago. The first in this series, No. 3460, was Santa Fe's only fully streamlined steam locomotive. It was a stylish machine, shrouded in lightweight steel with a bullet nose and skirting below the running boards. It was painted a subtle two-tone blue with an 18-inch stainless-steel band on the sides that read "Santa Fe" with the road number and silver leaf striping.

Milwaukee Road's *Hiawathas*

In the 1930s Milwaukee Road was one of three roads competing for passengers in the Chicago–Twin Cities corridor. Each of the three railroads took their own approach to speeding up schedules, but Milwaukee's story is exceptional. Rather than embrace diesel technology like rival Burlington, Milwaukee's *Hiawatha*

continued on page 86

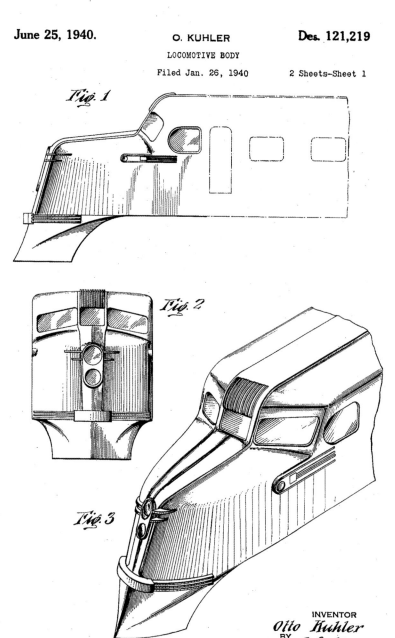

Otto Kuhler's design patent for the locomotive body used by Alco for its DL103 to DL109 road diesels. *United States Design Patent, 121,219, June 25, 1940*

Overleaf: Delivered in 1935, Milwaukee Road's A1 Atlantics were the first American streamlined steam locomotives built new. Milwaukee bought four of them. In this view No. 2 departs Chicago with the *Hiawatha* for its 410-mile run via Milwaukee to the Twin Cities. They were capable of sustained high-speed running and routinely cruised at 100-plus miles per hour. *Vernon Seaver, Jay Williams collection*

The popularity of the *Hiawatha* encouraged Milwaukee Road to run longer consists, and these required more power, so the railroad returned to Alco for more powerful streamlined *Hudsons*. These were styled by Otto Kuhler and included a vestibule cab for improved visibility. *John E. Pickett collection*

---

continued from page 83
steam locomotive emerged in response to the diesel, and as a result, became one of the most impressive steam trains on the planet.

Key to operating high-speed services is a high power-to-weight ratio. However in contrast to prevailing philosophies elsewhere that focused on building larger and more powerful locomotives to move heavier trains, Milwaukee reversed the equation and designed a substantially *lighter* passenger train, thus making it possible to use a comparatively small, yet very fast locomotive. Milwaukee pioneered lightweight passenger car design but opted to use highly refined conventional steam power to run at exceptional speeds. Before ordering new steam it made a test run. On July 20, 1934, it raced conventionally designed 4-6-4 No. 6402 from Chicago to Milwaukee in 67 minutes 35 seconds, making an average speed over a distance 68.9 miles of nearly 90 miles per hour.

The railroad wanted to introduce fast trains quickly, so it built equipment with minimal complexity that could be operated on the existing route with minimal requirements to upgrade plant or signaling,

while maintaining flexibility to adjust consists without the limitations associated with articulation.

Karl. F. Nystrom, a Swedish immigrant with a long history in the railroad industry, was the key designer of Milwaukee's lightweight streamlined cars. Having hired on with Milwaukee in 1922, from the late 1920s onward he was effectively Milwaukee's chief car builder. An article in March 1942 *Railway Mechanical Engineer* highlighted Nystrom's talent and Milwaukee's innovation: "Not only did the railroad design the cars, but the entire technique of building

continued on page 90

Overleaf: Near-cousins to Milwaukee's A-class Atlantics were Canadian Pacific Railway's semi-streamlined Jubilee types. These were technologically similar, despite differences in styling and CPR's 4-4-4-wheel arrangement. Like the A-class Atlantics, the Canadian locomotives were designed to haul lightweight cars and featured a large firebox, high boiler pressure, lightweight reciprocating parts, and Boxpok drivers. The first five were built by Alco's Canadian affiliate Montreal Locomotive Works, while others such as 2911 pictured were products of Canadian Locomotive Company Limited. *Canadian Pacific, Richard J. Solomon collection*

CHICAGO
MILWAUKEE
ST. PAUL
AND PACIFIC

Cited for distinguished service...

THE *Hiawathas*

TWIN CITIES
Hiawathas

2 a day, each way, serving

**CHICAGO • MILWAUKEE
LA CROSSE • WINONA
ST. PAUL • MINNEAPOLIS**

MIDWEST
Hiawatha

A fast, daytime schedule serving

**CHICAGO • DUBUQUE
CEDAR RAPIDS • DES MOINES
OMAHA • SIOUX CITY
SIOUX FALLS**

For schedules see tables 1, 7, 8, 9

IN the past four years, scores of civilians and service men alike have written to The Milwaukee Road commending HIAWATHA service. Overburdened as our trains were with a volume of travel that is still at record proportions, these great Speedliners consistently maintained high standards of speed and efficiency.

While the job of the railroads in returning veterans is still far from over, there are indications that the peak should soon be passed. We hope then to restore the extra measure of luxury that distinguished the HIAWATHAS. In the meantime, there's no better way to travel than on these great Speedliners.

H. Sengstacken, Assistant Passenger Traffic Manager
F. N. Hicks, Passenger Traffic Manager
Chicago

This January 1946 Milwaukee Road ad contrasts the Kuhler-styled F7 Hudson with an Electro-Motive E6A, locomotives that worked side by side for a decade. By 1946, Milwaukee had expanded its *Hiawatha* branding across a whole family of streamlined trains serving cities across its midwestern empire. *Solomon collection*

continued from page 86
them had to be developed, in order successfully to manufacture them in its shops."

By using welded construction and innovative structural design, Nystrom achieved weight reduction with conventional materials. Nystrom's prototype lightweight passenger coach emerged from the shops in May 1934, making it among the earliest streamlined lightweight passenger cars in the United States. At the time it was sent for display at the Century of Progress Exposition. Later that year, Milwaukee built cars using similar construction for revenue service, and these were the basis for its fast *Hiawatha* service. They weighed a third less than conventional steel-riveted cars. The back of the consists featured aerodynamic "beaver-tail," wedge-shaped observation cars

In developing its fast motive power, Milwaukee proved to be a total maverick. It worked with Alco but avoided the most radical innovative steam technology, such as the water-tube boilers embraced by Baltimore & Ohio. Notably it selected the obsolete 4-4-2 Atlantic-type that it had perfected in the early years of the twentieth century, which it deemed still ideally suited for very fast operation. It did embrace innovations made possible by improved metallurgy, as well as modern roller-bearing technology that suited its desire for speed, power, and simplicity. To the casual observer, it was their stunning appearance that separated Milwaukee's Atlantics from everything else on the rails.

Although New York Central had earlier experimented with modern wind-resistant streamlined shrouds on a steam locomotive in the United States, true aerodynamic tests of shrouds were first performed by Norman Zapf, an engineering graduate student at the then Case School of Applied Science in Cleveland. Donald J. Bush, in *The Streamlined Decade*, states that Zapf performed wind-tunnel tests on a model of a New York Central Hudson-type demonstrating that aerodynamic shrouds would reduce wind drag and thus improve locomotive output. While New York Central applied wind-resistant shrouds to J-1 Hudson No. 5344 by December 1934, nevertheless Milwaukee's Atlantics were the first newly built streamlined steam locomotives.

Milwaukee's streamlining shrouds followed aerodynamic principles as applied to both New York Central 5344 and Burlington's shovelnosed *Zephyr*. *Railway Mechanical Engineer* reported in December 1935 that during mid-1934 Alco, along with ACF and J. G. Brill, jointly conducted wind-tunnel tests at New York University to compare the relative wind resistance of various shapes and patterns.

Milwaukee's desire for streamlining was as much a consideration of public perception as its need to reduce wind resistance. Its *Hiawatha* needed to both look like it would go fast as well as to actually travel quickly. Its motif therefore blended state-of-the-art aerodynamic treatment with unique, distinctive styling.

To distinguish the *Hiawatha* from ordinary passenger trains, Milwaukee boldly painted both locomotives using bright colors in place of the traditional black locomotive and Pullman-green cars. These were decorated in a gray, orange, and maroon livery with stylized silver wings wrapped around the front of the locomotive. High headlight placement at the top of the locomotive, bracketed by stylized air-intake vents, and a steeply pitched 16-degree, shovelnose profile with wrap-around pilot and flared skirting over the lead-wheels hinted at the recently debuted *Zephyr*.

The shrouds were made from a steel frame mounted on the running boards that completely covered the top and sides of the boiler and related appliances. They extended down nearly another 3 feet below the running boards to conceal reverse gear, valve gear, and water pumps, yet left driving wheels open for maintenance and inspection.

Milwaukee ordered the first two Atlantics from Alco in October 1934. These were delivered to Milwaukee on May 5, 1935, designated Class A, and numbered 1 and 2, to impart their significance. As business swelled, Alco built two additional Class A Atlantics; No. 3 in 1936 and No. 4 in 1937.

Initially the Atlantics hauled five- and six-car *Hiawatha* consists, but as the *Hiawatha* grew in popularity the railroad adjusted the size of the train; soon seven-car trains of lightweight cars were necessary. When traffic demands exceeded the abilities of the fast Atlantics: Milwaukee turned to Alco for a more powerful steam locomotive.

Alco delivered six highly refined, elegant streamlined Hudsons to Milwaukee in August 1938, designated as Class F7 (not to be confused with the common Electro-Motive F7 diesel-electric). The shrouding displayed distinctive flare that is credited as the joint work of Milwaukee's engineers, Alco, and industrial designer Otto Kuhler, who worked on a

Southern Pacific train 99, the *Daylight* seen with streamlined-styled Lima-built GS2 4412 with Pullman cars on the Coast Line circa 1938. SP's *Daylight* was one of the most successful 1930s streamliners. *Jay Williams collection*

variety of Alco's designs. The F7's boilers had ample capacity to maintain sustained high speed with long consists.

Milwaukee's A class Atlantics and F7 Hudsons are remembered as *the* fastest regularly scheduled steam locomotives in the world. No other steam locomotives ran so quickly on a day-to-day basis. To maintain *Hiawatha*'s regular schedule these routinely cruised in excess of 100 miles per hour. Some estimates indicated they operated faster than 110 miles per hour, and on occasion may have touched the 120-miles-per-hour mark or faster.

The exclusive reign of steam on *Hiawatha* ended in 1941 when Milwaukee bought its first passenger diesels: an A-B pair of Electro-Motive model E6s and an A-B set of Otto Kuhler–style Alco DL-109s. Milwaukee expanded its *Hiawatha* concept into a whole family of similarly styled trains, serving a variety of destinations across its system.

Southern Pacific *Daylight*

In 1933, Angus McDonald became president of Southern Pacific and encouraged new ideas that might boost passenger ridership. SP hired ad agency Lord & Thomas to study the problem. Among their suggestions was offering lower fares combined with better advertising, while implementing European-style high-speed internal combustion railcars to improve the Oakland-Sacramento service.

Richard K. Wright in *Southern Pacific Daylight* wrote that only a few months after the *Flying Hamburger* entered revenue service in September

continued on page 94

Chicago & North Western's nine streamlined Alco class E-4 4-6-4 Hudsons were built to handle transcontinental passenger services operated in conjunction with Union Pacific, including the *Overland Limited* and *Pacific Limited*. These powerful and fast locomotives were built to the same specifications as Milwaukee Road's F-7s. C&NW's engines

featured a subdued streamlining treatment, painted in traditional Pullman green with elegant gold striping. They were high-capacity machines that routinely hauled ten- to eighteen-car trains on express schedules between Chicago and Omaha. Larger tenders minimized the need for fuel and water stops. *R. H. Carlson, Jay Williams collection*

New Haven's *Comet* was a unique train; not only was it the only double-ended articulated diesel streamliner, but it was the only train built by the American-German joint venture Goodyear-Zeppelin, a company that primarily made airships at its Akron, Ohio, facility. The *Comet* is seen at speed on the Shoreline route, where it made up to six roundtrips daily between Boston and Providence. *Robert A. Buck collection*

continued from page 91
1933 SP's Charles L. Eggelston proposed an advanced three-piece railcar design to McDonald. But this design, which closely resembled the German railcars, didn't appeal to McDonald who wanted a luxurious streamlined train rather than a functional lightweight speedster. McDonald instead encouraged SP's mechanical department under George McCormick to refine a luxury streamliner for SP's prestigious Coast route.

In 1936 SP planned for a plush streamliner for the San Francisco–Los Angeles run. George McCormick's team contracted Pullman for construction of an all-new lightweight, streamlined train hauled by powerful refined steam locomotives.

Pullman supplied low-center-of-gravity, lightweight cars that benefited from SP input to blend new technologies and concepts with conventional designs. Car bodies were made of Cor-Ten steel with welded truss-style side framing using vertical and diagonal supports. These featured the cosmetic application of corrugated stainless-steel side sheathing to resemble Budd-style equipment. On Pullman's recommendation, SP ordered pairs of articulated coaches that shared a common center truck but with conventional end couplers. These had the advantage of reduced tare weight without unnecessarily compromising flexibility. Car ends were fitted with center and outer diaphragms to make the cars visually seamless, giving the train the appearance of streamlined continuity rather than a group of separate cars.

The styling of the new *Daylight* train involved a flashy new red, orange, and black paint scheme—the orange matched the hue of California's poppy while the overall golden connotation alluded to the nineteenth-century Gold Rush, with California, of course, being the "Golden State." Eggleston designed a stylized *Daylight* insignia while Pullman and Southern Pacific designers collaborated on details of interior styling where subdued colors complemented the trains' flashy exterior. Secondary ceiling lighting provided a soft overall glow, while spotlights were positioned over each seat for reading and direct illumination to give the train a modern ambiance.

To lead the *Daylight*, Southern Pacific ordered six semi-streamlined "Superpower" 4-8-4s from the Lima

Locomotive Works of Lima, Ohio, that were among the most modern locomotives of their kind. These stunning machines caught the eye of everyone who saw them; dressed to match the passenger cars made them the most colorful locomotives on Southern Pacific. The locomotives' "streamlining" was solely to fulfill aesthetic ideals: boiler casing enclosed eternal locomotive piping, sand domes, steam dome, smoke stack, and related equipment. However, they didn't feature overall sheathing that concealed the shape of the locomotive as did earlier streamlined steam, such as New York Central's *Commodore Vanderbilt*. Neat skirting extended from pilot to cab along the running boards, while the headlight was encased in the stream-style housing centered on the smokebox door. Rather than traditional spoked driving wheels, these used those of latest cast-steel Boxpok design.

Southern Pacific proudly launched its new streamlined *Daylights* with joint ceremonies at San Francisco and Los Angeles on March 21, 1937, to christen the trains—SP executives, movie stars, and the public joined in celebration. The pair of sleek twelve-car trains had cost $1 million, making them the most expensive new trains debuted to date. Each set had capacity for 584 revenue passengers.

Daylight Success

Southern Pacific's colorful *Daylights* were an immediate success with the public. By July 1937, SP was advertising that the train had carried 62,899 passengers in its first three months and was averaging 342 passengers daily in each direction. By the end of the first full year, the *Daylights* were the most heavily traveled single-section train in the United States.

Within a year of *Daylight*'s debut, SP planned for more *Daylights* and ordered an additional fourteen Lima 4-8-4s of a refined design and more passenger cars for longer consists. Among the novelties were three-unit articulated dining cars that featured 152 seats. New *Daylight* consists entered service on January 10, 1940, as the *Morning Daylight*. The 1937 trains were refurbished, modified, and reassigned to a new service called the *Noon Daylight*, which began operation on March 30, 1940. SP continued to expand the concept and introduced the *San Joaquin Daylight* to the San Joaquin Valley route via Bakersfield on Independence Day 1941 (yet this train didn't become a full streamliner until 1942).

A 1938 advertisement for New Haven's one-of-a-kind streamlined *Comet* that connected Boston and Providence with multiple daily trips. *Solomon collection*

SP also completely re-equipped its premier overnight coast train, known as the *Lark*, with a streamlined consist on par with the *Daylights* that was inaugurated on May 1, 1941. This embraced a similar styling, but used subdued two-tone gray-and-black livery: car bodies were neutral gray, the window section was treated with a darker bluish gray and highlighted with white pinstripes, while the roof was dressed in glossy black. Each train carried thirteen all-bedroom Pullmans, but its most stunning car was the three-segment, articulated *Lark Club* dining-lounge. Interior decor included stylish engraved illuminated glass panels, soft fluorescent lighting, and a mix of pastel colors. It was advertised as "One of the most beautiful trains in America."

New Haven's *Comet*

An anomaly among American diesel streamliners was New Haven Railroad's one-of-a-kind *Comet*. This more closely followed the pattern established by European

New Haven's *Comet* approaches its terminus at Providence; the Rhode Island Capitol building is perched on the hill to the left of the train. *Comet* was designed for a relatively short run and rapid turnaround at terminals, thus the desire for a double-ended train. *Robert A. Buck collection*

diesel railcars than the other early American articulated trains. Unlike western streamliners built for long-distance luxury services, the *Comet* was conceived for short-distance travel and was built as a double-ended train to facilitate rapid turn-around at terminals, with 400-horsepower six-cylinder, inline four-cycle Westinghouse engines at both ends. It was the only American double-ended, aerodynamically designed, multicar, streamlined diesel train.

A Westinghouse ad read: "Balanced power—a Diesel-electric plant at each end—gives smoother operation and eliminates necessity of turning train at terminals."

The ad was a futile last gasp for Westinghouse's diesel program. Although it had been among America's diesel-electric pioneers, New Haven's *Comet* was one of its last independent commercial diesel efforts. After Electro-Motive's entrance into the commercial locomotive market, Westinghouse joined forces with Baldwin as its electrical supplier for commercial

primarily facilitated construction of airships in the United States. However, by the mid-1930s, the collapse of the Zeppelin airship market led the Goodyear-Zeppelin consortium to try building streamlined trains as a way of increasing its business. *Comet* was its sole effort.

Railway Age profiled the train in its April 27, 1935, issue, detailing its construction and suppliers. *Comet*'s aerodynamic shape was the product of wind-tunnel experiments conducted by the Daniel Guggenheim Airship Institute in Akron, Ohio. It used a tubular-aluminum design with riveted construction. Goodyear-Zeppelin delivered the *Comet* to New Haven in April 1935, just a year after the debut of the similarly shaped Budd stainless-steel *Zephyr*. Like *Zephyr* and UP's M-10000, and various European trains, it was an articulated, three-car, low-profile train. *Comet* measured 207 feet long, and passenger cars were 11 feet 3 inches over the rail. It was capable of 110 miles per hour and designed for sustained 90-miles-per-hour operation. The exterior paint scheme was jointly designed by New Haven and the Sherwin-Williams Paint Company, featuring prominent blue striping. The interior was simple and functional: walls with three shades of tan, and a pink-tinted ceiling lit by uniform indirect lighting. The paint company featured the *Comet* in its advertising that read "Comet . . . streamline! . . . speed!"

Following a high-profile Boston to New Haven test run, *Comet* entered service as intended between Boston and Providence, where it was initially scheduled to make five roundtrips daily, beginning and ending each day at Providence. It ran a one-way trip in just 44 minutes, averaging nearly 60 miles per hour start to stop, which was more than 10 minutes quicker than the best contemporary steam schedule. White wrote that the train turned 405,000 miles in its first three years of service. New Haven scrapped it in 1951.

Otto Kuhler's Lehigh Valley Streamliners

In 1938, new Lehigh Valley president Duncan Kerr contracted industrial designer Otto Kuhler to restyle the railroad's passenger trains to boost ridership. Kuhler's first project was a gas-electric, which he improved using a sophisticated modern black-and-orange paint scheme to signify the colors of a coal fire—LV being a major anthracite hauler. The car entered service in November 1938.

continued on page 100

diesel construction and ceased construction of its own diesel-electrics.

New Haven had ordered the *Comet* from the Goodyear-Zeppelin Corporation in 1934, and it was intended to make the sprint from Boston's South Station to Providence, a distance of just 43.25 miles. John White Jr. notes in *The American Railroad Passenger Car* that the railroad financed its purchase using a Public Works Administration loan (which make the train an early example of federal investment to improve service on the Northeast Corridor route).

Goodyear-Zeppelin was an interwar joint venture between American and German companies that

continued on page 100

RAYMOND LOEWY

by Brian Solomon

French-born Raymond Loewy (1893–1986) was one of the great drivers in the field of industrial design and a streamlining pioneer. His was among the most famous names attached to American railway streamlining. Where other designers of the streamlined era were employees of larger companies and were rarely publicly credited for their design work, Loewy owned his design firm and went to great efforts to publicize his work.

Loewy served in a French artillery unit during World War I; he managed to survive the war intact and was decorated for his service. His parents died in the great influenza epidemic after the war, which led him to immigrate to America. He worked in illustration and graphic design, and by the mid-1920s he was recognized as among the foremost artists of the Paris art deco school. In 1929 he moved into industrial design, a new field that he helped define.

An unabashed railway enthusiast, Loewy's desire to design locomotives was as much a delight as an assignment. As early as 1911, he had sketched locomotives and in his later years recalled the pleasure of being around trains in his youth. In his 1937 book, *The Locomotive,* which promoted his design ideals and offered biased criticism of contemporary railway designs while showcasing his own efforts, he wrote, "My youth was charmed by the glamour of the locomotive. I am still under its spell and in this volume I rather write about the beauty of the magnificent creature to which I owe some of my most cherished souvenirs."

Loewy's design philosophy embraced smooth surfaces and minimal embellishment. He espoused simplicity and restraint. Paul Jodard in his biography, *Raymond Loewy Design Hero,* quoted Loewy on design:

Raymond Loewy's first full-scale locomotive streamlining project was his shrouding work for Pennsylvania Railroad K4s Pacific 3768 in 1937 (the small letter 's' indicates "superheat"). Loewy and New York University conducted more than 100 wind-tunnel tests using scale models to devise the aerodynamic shape of the locomotive. Streamlined K4s 3768 is seen posed with one of its nonshrouded sisters at Zoo Junction in Philadelphia. *Bob's Photos collection*

"[It is] a simple exercise—a little logic, a little taste and the will to co-operate." As Loewy gained fame and success, his firm hired teams of assistants and associates. He had a dozen employees in 1935, and 75 a decade later. Yet, Loewy's name always predominated. Through skillful promotion and media manipulation he gradually built a reputation as head of one of America's foremost design firms. He exuded charm, personally courted top clients, and brushed elbows with celebrities.

His designs went well beyond railroads; he was involved in the improvement of everything from small machinery and household items to architecture, ships, corporate insignias, and NASA's Skylab interiors. Among his most famous commissions was the Lucky Strike cigarette package, a Coca-Cola soda fountain, and Studebaker automobiles, including the Avanti sports coupe of 1962.

Pennsylvania's S1 streamlined *Duplex* was unlike anything else that came before it and was intended to rival the most modern diesel power and to awe the public. It could easily haul a heavy passenger train at 100 miles per hour. While its inspiring appearance and enormous power were impressive, the colossal *Duplex* was a tremendous flop. It lacked the flexibility and low operational costs afforded by diesels, and was too limited for service because of its great length. *Robert A. Buck collection*

Loewy's prolific resumé and artful self-promotion didn't always earn him favor among his contemporaries. Yet, his success paved the way for the entire field of industrial design. Jodard reported that Loewy's contemporary Henry Dreyfuss, known for his designs of New York Central streamliners, begrudgingly acknowledged Loewy's fame: "We all know about Raymond Loewy (and publicity) but let's not forget that he is the best advertisement this profession has: without him the profession would be very different." Jodard cautioned that Loewy had a reputation for design claims "some of them quite outrageously wrong." In the summer 2009 *Classic Trains*, Hampton C. Wayt explored the design of Pennsylvania Railroad's GG1, producing considerable evidence that while Loewy was involved with the locomotive's design, much of the work often attributed to Loewy was in fact the work of Westinghouse designer Donald Dohner.

Yet, it was Loewy's early participation in railroad design that contributed to his professional success. In 1933, he earned a minor commission from the Pennsylvania Railroad to produce an improved trash can design for New York's Penn Station. This small task gave him an audience with PRR's President Theodore Clement. Soon Loewy was given more prestigious assignments, including the contentious job of tidying up the GG1.

PRR later gave Loewy a greater hand in improving the company's style, work that included designing the interiors for its new streamlined *Broadway Limited*, and providing streamlining for K4s Pacific 3768. He poured his heart into this locomotive. Working with PRR's Engineering department and New York University, Loewy explained in *The Locomotive* that he conducted more than 100 wind-tunnel tests to perfect his design and minimize air resistance while channeling exhaust gases away from the locomotive cab. Among Loewy's pet peeves were extraneous appendages such as "elephant ear"-style smoke lifters that he felt spoiled the appearance of locomotives.

His work on 3768 led to an even more ambitious streamlining exercise. Among Loewy's most famous creations was PRR's massive S1 *Duplex* of 1939, a unique machine that has become an emblem of the whole streamlining movement. The engine gained public notice through its prominent display at the New York World's Fair in 1939 and 1940 where it was portrayed as the future of railroad motive power. Although PRR's "Big Engine" proved to be too big for most applications, the scaled-down version of the *Duplex* concept, PRR's T1 discussed in Chapter 4, also featured a distinctive Loewy streamlined treatment.

In this Pennsylvania Railroad advertisement, Raymond Loewy's ship-prow-style T1 made for an alternative vision of the future. When many railroads were considering Electro-Motive diesels, PRR pursued a nonconventional motive-power approach and bought a fleet of high-speed *Duplex* steam locomotives. Although fast, powerful, and impressively streamlined, the T1s suffered from early technical flaws and couldn't match the economy offered by new diesels. *Solomon collection*

Lehigh Valley applied Otto Kuhler's streamlined shrouds to five of its Pacifics. This was one of the later three engines that was streamlined for *The Black Diamond* and featured a nominally more conservative treatment. Compare the front of this locomotive with that of Lehigh Valley 2102 (below right) with its lateral wrap-around fins below the bullet nose and the fan of vertical fins in front of the smokestack. *Robert A. Buck collection*

continued from page 97

Kuhler then focused on a nominal restyling of Lehigh Valley's *Asa Packer* service. Although neither of these initial economy efforts can be considered streamlining, it led to Kuhler's more significant work styling LV's *The John Wilkes*. This train connected New York City with the Pennsylvania city of Wilkes-Barre (named in honor of eighteenth-century British politicians John Wilkes and Isaac Barré). Kuhler collaborated with Lehigh Valley motive-power superintendent, J. P. Laux, in the application of elaborate sheet-metal shrouds to a pair of elderly Baldwin-built class K-5 Pacifics (Nos. 2101 and 2102). In addition to shrouding, these were modernized with lightweight reciprocating rods and Boxpok driving wheels. Work was carried out at the Sayre, Pennsylvania, shops. On the advice of President Kerr, Kuhler designed a Cornell red-and-black paint scheme, augmenting these sedate colors

with white striping and stainless-steel handrails. The futuristic effect made the locomotives seem like they were racing at great speed even when at a standstill.

Kuhler applied an equivalent exterior treatment to the passenger cars refurbished for *The John Wilkes*, and redecorated the interiors in shades of green with stainless-steel trimming and fluorescent lighting. In April 1939, before it entered regular service, Lehigh Valley gave employees a chance to experience the new stream-styled *The John Wilkes* set with an excursion along Seneca Lake in central New York State.

Lehigh Valley's final Kuhler project was styling its re-equipped flagship train, *The Black Diamond*. The railroad ordered ten new Pullman lightweight coaches built at its Osgood Bradley plant in Worcester, Massachusetts. Kuhler applied a similar streamlined treatment to three additional Pacifics (two were Alco-built, the third was a home-built machine); however the frontal treatment was slightly different than the first two locomotives and featured a curved plate over the lateral fins below the bullet nose with a single vertical fin lined up below the headlight.

Lehigh Valley's streamliners were among the most distinctive in the eastern United States, but Kuhler's full styling treatment was short-lived. The complexity of the sheet metal combined with the strains of

Lehigh Valley 2097 was a fifteen-year old Alco product when it was shrouded at the railroad's Sayre, Pennsylvania, shops for service on its flagship passenger train, *The Black Diamond*, which sprinted daily over the length of the railroad connecting New York City and Buffalo. Lehigh Valley was primarily an anthracite coal carrier but prided itself by running some very classy passenger trains. *John E. Pickett collection*

Lehigh Valley 2102 is an old Pacific type in a fresh new dress. On September 17, 1939, it pauses at Bethlehem, Pennsylvania, with *The John Wilkes*, Lehigh Valley's day-train running from Wilkes Barre, Pennsylvania, to Penn Station, New York. This was one of two Baldwin Pacific's streamlined by Otto Kuhler for the train. Later he applied a slightly different shrouding for three more Pacifics assigned to *The Black Diamond*. *John E. Pickett collection*

To overcome the safety hazards associated with its front-end boxcab electrics, Pennsylvania Railroad adopted Donald Dohner's center-cab streamlined design for its final order of P5A electrics. These were classified as "P5A Modified" and in their early years worked passenger trains as intended but were largely reassigned to freight service as PRR received more GG1s. Like the prototype GG1, these electrics featured riveted skin. *James Bowie, Robert A. Buck collection*

World War II resulted in pieces of shrouding gradually being removed from the locomotives. By the end of the war, the Pacifics exhibited a more sedate appearance that lacked the flare of Kuhler's intended treatment. Alco-GE PA passenger diesels came in the late 1940s, and the Pacifics were shorn of remaining streamlined shrouds and briefly reassigned to other duties before scrapping.

Pennsylvania's GG1

Pennsylvania Railroad's renowned streamlined GG1 was America's most famous electric locomotive. In its classic form, it wore Brunswick green with five gold pinstriped "cats whiskers," which was the face of the railroad's acclaimed New York–Washington mainline electrification (the most extensive project of its kind in North America, and the nation's premier passenger route). The GG1 was made famous by its prominence

on passenger trains serving two of America's largest cities and its capital, its primary role in advertising, and the showcase treatment by toy train manufacturer Lionel in its postwar O-scale models, coveted by a generation of young railway enthusiasts.

The GG1 seemed to represent the perfect fusion of speed, power, and modern streamlined style. While the GG1 appeared on the scene within months of Union Pacific's *Streamliner* and Burlington's *Zephyr*, the story of its creation isn't as straightforward as other streamliners. This was a solution for previous design failures with PRR's initial electric locomotives for its New York–Washington project. Its streamlining wasn't the work of one visionary designer but a compromise executed by various people.

Pennsylvania Railroad was America's largest railroad and had a long history of doing things its own way. The railroad was among the first to embrace electrification, although early efforts used direct current third rail, PRR later emerged as a pioneer of the high-voltage, alternating current overhead system, which offered greater efficiency over long distances. In 1928 PRR announced ambitious plans to electrify its busy New York City–Washington, D.C. route, including branches, secondary mainlines, as well as its east/west "Main Line" between Philadelphia and Harrisburg, Pennsylvania. These routes accommodated hundreds of long-distance and suburban passenger trains and freight trains daily. It continued this project despite the onset of the Great Depression; however completion of the project required that the PRR accept significant financial assistance from the federal government.

PRR engineering forces designed a fleet of Spartan-looking boxcab electrics based on its most successful steam locomotive wheel arrangements but arranged in a dual-cab, bi-directional format. The most successful of these was the P5 and P5a, which used the 2-C-2-wheel arrangement based on the enormously successful 4-6-2 Pacific.

By 1933, PRR's boxcabs were proving inadequate for high-speed passenger service. They suffered both from engineering flaws and insufficient power. PRR investigated other solutions and borrowed a New Haven EP-3 boxcab that featured the 2-C+C-2 articulated wheel arrangement for testing.

As PRR was refining its locomotive design in early 1934, a disastrous grade-crossing accident in New Jersey that killed a locomotive engineer demonstrated the dangers of front end-cab design. This encouraged design of a completely new style of electric locomotive. By January 1934, PRR decided to build two prototypes: the GG1 patterned on the New Haven electric wheel arrangement; and an R1, based on the 4-8-4 steam locomotive. PRR worked with Baldwin and Westinghouse in this prototype development.

To avoid the obvious flaws of an unprotected end cab, PRR adopted an elevated center-cab design, which had its origins in New York Central's third-rail electrics of 1904–1905, and later used on PRR's L5 electrics of the World War I period. Hampton C. Wayt, writing about the early GG1 development in *Classic Trains*, details the crucial role of Westinghouse Electric &

Pennsylvania Railroad's riveted-body prototype GG1 leads a group of its production sisters that featured welded skin. PRR No. 4800 was affectionately known as "Old Rivets" and enjoyed a working career that spanned more than four decades. *Jim Shaughnessy*

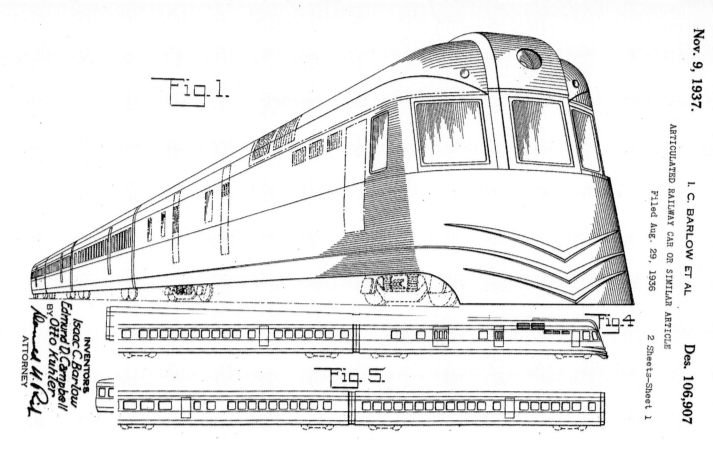

Above & Opposite: This design patent issued to Isaac C. Barlow, Edmund D. Campbell, and Otto Kuhler, reflects the basic shape applied to Gulf, Mobile & Northern's *Rebel* streamlined trains built by ACF. Although the patent specifies an "articulated railway car," ACF's trains for GM&N were not articulated. *United States Design Patent No. 106,907, Nov. 9, 1937*

Manufacturing Company's industrial designer, Donald Dohner, a man whose name had long been left out of the streamlining story.

According to Wayt, Dohner was a highly regarded design specialist, who in 1930 was appointed to head Westinghouse's new Art in Engineering department. Among his credentials was development of Westinghouse's "Visibility Cab" for its diesel-electric switchers. Dohner worked on the GG1 from the early days of the project and made six different plaster models showing variations of streamlined design. These defined the essential shape of the locomotive and anticipated a variety of details in the final design, including side striping, the front door mounted headlight, and a smooth skin appearance with compound curves. This streamlined treatment was applied to PRR's prototypes and on an additional group of twenty-eight P5A electrics, designated "P5A modified" to distinguish them from the earlier boxcabs.

The modified P5A design caught the attention of *Railway Age*, which focused on the redesigned cab in a detailed description published on July 28, 1934. The new cab arrangement gave the electric engine "more symmetry of line," and "each end of the new locomotive will slope gently inward from the floor to the cab roof, with rounded shoulders running toward the central operating compartment." *Railway Age* found the improved P5A to be "generally more attractive and pleasing to the eye."

Extensive testing in 1934 between the two prototypes led PRR to choose the GG1 with its articulated wheel arrangement for mass production. By the end of 1934 Dohner had left Westinghouse and PRR hired Raymond Loewy to further refine the GG1's appearance. Historically, Loewy has been credited with the introduction of a seamless welded skin, instead of the crude riveted skin used on the prototype (engine 4899, later renumbered 4800, and colloquially known as "Old Rivets"), and of the introduction of the classy, five-stripe "cat's whiskers" paint scheme—later adapted for PRR's passenger diesels. Though Wayt casts doubt on some of these details, he acknowledges Loewy's involvement in the project. Today Dohner's role in the GG1 has been recognized, and he is considered, along with Loewy, to be among the fathers of American industrial design.

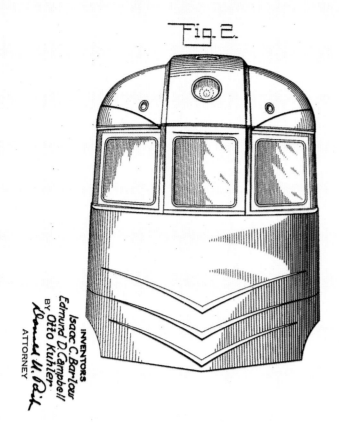

Nov. 9, 1937.   Des. 106,907

I. C. BARLOW ET AL

ARTICULATED RAILWAY CAR OR SIMILAR ARTICLE

Filed Aug. 29, 1936   2 Sheets-Sheet 2

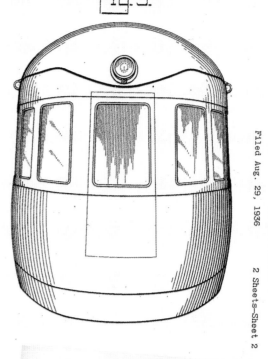

Electric service between New York and Washington began in February 1935, and by mid-1935 PRR was operating a fleet of 57 GG1s, including the prototype. Not only was this the largest fleet of mass-produced streamlined locomotives in North America, it outnumbered all the other combined streamlining efforts at that time. The GG1 remained in production until 1943, by which time PRR had assembled a fleet of 139 GG1s. Many outlasted the railroad, which merged with New York Central in 1968, with the final GG1 operations concluded in October 1983, more than forty-nine years after they began.

American Car & Foundry Streamlined Railcars

By the mid-1930s the self-propelled multi-section streamlined railcar appeared to be on its way to becoming the new type of standard passenger train. This was a worldwide phenomenon. Germany's high-speed cars had set the standard in Europe, and that was quickly emulated by most of the industrialized European nations. By 1935, Belgium, Denmark, France, and the Netherlands were among countries operating diesel railcar streamliners, and railways in South America and Asia were also quick to adopt the new style.

American Car & Foundry was a significant railcar manufacturer that aimed to develop this new diesel concept. In 1935, Isaac B. Tigrett's recently formed

The parallel Mobile & Ohio and Gulf, Mobile & Northern systems were merged in 1940. This advertisement for Gulf, Mobile & Ohio's *Rebel* is from the railroad's January 1941 public timetable and was designed to entice travelers to experience the streamlined train. Don't you wish you were the lucky guy in the photograph? *Solomon collection*

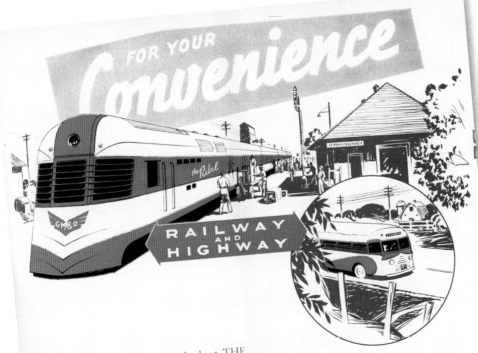

Left: American Car & Foundry built Gulf, Mobile & Northern's streamlined trains, which were powered by Alco diesel engines. *Solomon collection*

Below: Compared with its freight trains, Gulf, Mobile & Northern's svelte streamlined *Rebel* appeared as the vision of modern railroading. Yet, while the new trains revived its long-distance passenger services, it was freights like that pictured at the bottom of this 1938 advertisement that paid the bills. *Solomon collection*

Next time you plan a trip ask about THE REBEL ROUTE . . . for throughout a great part of Gulf, Mobile and Ohio's territory, your railroad ticket buys you a double service . . . a service entitling you to ride either our trains or our buses or whatever combination of the two is most convenient for you.

G. M. & O.'s highway operation is by its subsidiary Gulf Transport Company, and tickets are interchangeable between points served by both trains and buses.

Passengers may go on the bus and return on the train or vice versa . . . according to the convenience of the schedules.

We know you will like this double service. Buses are as modern as our stream-liners. Drivers are safe and courteous and in many instances buses and trains arrive and depart from the same stations.

DON'T FORGET NEXT TIME ASK ABOUT G. M. & O.'S
CONVENIENT COMBINATION

Gulf, Mobile & Northern system (a railroad melded together from lines connecting St. Louis with cities in the Deep South) ordered a pair of streamlined trains from ACF using federal loans made possible through the Public Works Administration. GM&N desired a modern train to reduce operating costs and attract passengers back to the rails. It had no need for high-speed trains and was satisfied with a functional trainset that could nominally improve running times over conventional steam power.

ACF's Berwick, Pennsylvania, shops built two four-piece trains powered by Alco diesels for GM&N's new *Rebels* service. In *The American Railroad Passenger Car* John H. White described these as "solid, practical, devoid of foolish experiments." Like other streamliners, these had a low profile, measuring just over 11 feet 7 inches above the rail. Cars were made from

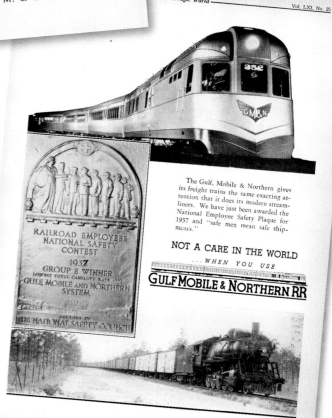

The Traffic World — Vol. LXI. No. 25

The Gulf, Mobile & Northern gives its freight trains the same exacting attention that it does its modern streamliners. We have just been awarded the National Employee Safety Plaque for 1937 and "safe men mean safe shipments."

NOT A CARE IN THE WORLD
. . . WHEN YOU USE
GULF MOBILE & NORTHERN RR

Gulf, Mobile & Ohio January 1941 timetable features one of
the railroad's distinctive prewar Kuhler-styled Alco road diesels.
Solomon collection

New Jersey's New York, Susquehanna & Western sampled American Car & Foundry's streamlined *Motorailers*. It bought two cars new in 1940 and a few years later picked up four more cars secondhand from Illinois Central. NYS&W 1003 was one of the former IC cars. NYS&W assigned the cars to its commuter services. *Photographer unknown, Robert A. Buck collection*

rust-resistant Cor-Ten steel, nominally lighter than conventional equipment but heavier than the earlier ultra-light concept trains, and they were not articulated (each car ran on its own pairs of four-wheel trucks). Otto Kuhler contributed to their styling, painted in a simple, but modern silver-and-red livery. GM&N ordered a third train in 1938. The *Rebels* worked as intended on the St. Louis–New Orleans run until the mid-1950s.

In 1940, ACF introduced its amply powered, semi-streamlined *Motorailer*, in anticipation of a mass-market for self-propelled cars on medium-distance routes. These were 76 feet long and powered by Brill engines. Although it was an innovative adaptation of the generation-old railcar, and aimed at reducing operating costs, ACF only found a few customers. New York, Susquehanna & Western bought a few for suburban services, while Illinois Central bought some for its secondary medium-distance runs. Missouri Pacific also sampled the cars, and some were sold

to South America. IC wasn't impressed and sold all of its cars to NYS&W. World War II appears to have killed *Motorailer* before it could get started, and these cars remained a little-remarked sideshow of the streamlined era.

Was Aerodynamic Design Necessary?

Between the 1920s and mid-1930s advanced automotive and aircraft designs inspired international interest in using wind-tunnel research to perfect aerodynamic streamlined forms for railway vehicles. But did aerodynamic design really make a difference to operations?

The desire for speed, combined with the association of increased speed with progress, propelled designers to propose a host of futuristic aerodynamic designs. Reducing air drag through the application of natural shapes, such as the teardrop combined with smooth surfaces and a minimal of protrusions, aimed to improve efficiency of modern vehicles operating at high speeds. Meanwhile the development of new materials and advanced manufacturing techniques made them practical and cost-effective to apply streamlined forms.

When they were introduced, experimental streamlined trains delighted the public and thrilled passengers, while changing the shape and construction
continued on page 112

LELAND A. KNICKERBOCKER

by John Gruber and Paul A. Meyer

D. C. 82—Streamlining thru Florida, America's Vacationland

In 1940, Illinois Central debuted the colorfully painted, diesel-hauled *City of Miami* streamliner that made a round trip every third day between its namesake and Chicago. It was operated in conjunction with Central of Georgia, Atlantic Coast Line and Florida East Coast. This stylized period postcard features IC 4000, an Electro-Motive E6A bought and specially painted for *City of Miami* service. The E6 was the final prewar Electro-Motive E-unit model, built between 1940 and 1942, and was supplanted by model E7 in 1945. *Solomon collection*

In the diesel locomotive's formative years, Electro-Motive's design and styling came from the same Detroit staff that styled automobiles. When the Electro-Motive Company in 1930 became a part of the giant family of General Motors companies, EMC had access to the GM Styling Group, led by Harley J. Earl (1893–1969), known for his use of tail fins and chrome trim.

The group, at the time called the GM Styling & Color Industrial Division, assigned Leland A. Knickerbocker (1893–1939) and Paul A. Meyer (1910–94) to EMC. Although it is very likely that other individuals were given temporary assignments to this group, especially in 1939 with Knickerbocker's untimely death, General Motors maintained control of all Electro-Motive styling until 1941 when EMC became a full division of General Motors and formed it's own Styling Group in La Grange.

Knickerbocker, born in Holley, New York, near Rochester, started his career as a book illustrator, painter, and sculptor in New York State. His earliest known work for EMC is a group of color paintings from 1934–35 showing proposals for 1,800-horsepower boxcab passenger locomotives. He designed the Rock Island's

Rocket paint scheme in 1936 and quickly followed with the most famous paint scheme of all time, the Santa Fe's red warbonnet in 1937.

Meyer, a graduate of the Cleveland School of Art, joined the GM staff in 1934, working primarily on Buick and Cadillac/LaSalle styling. Automobile affectionists remember him primarily for the 1938 Buick "Y-Job," the concept convertible that Earl drove for ten years. Meyer's name has been found on such famous paint schemes as the Illinois Central *City of Miami* in 1940 and the *Panama Limited* in 1941, which eventually evolved into the IC's orange and chocolate paint scheme.

In an age without fax machines or e-mail, design ideas were mailed back and forth between Detroit and LaGrange. Based upon the dates found on early styling proposals, EMD engineering drawing title blocks, and microfilm of the original order files, the GM Styling Group worked at least one year ahead of the engineers.

In addition to producing the many carbody design proposals for the development of the streamliner body style, the two men were also responsible for paint schemes for the scores of highly individualistic and competitive railroad companies.

Electro-Motive Pioneer FT set No. 103 demonstrated to American railroads the exceptional capabilities of diesels working in a variety of heavy services. It was arguably the most significant locomotive of the twentieth century. Although it was judged primarily by its performance, would it have been so successful if the FT had been built as nondescript black boxcab? *Brian Solomon*

Missouri Pacific's original *Eagle* ran from St. Louis to Omaha. It was soon developed into a whole family of similarly streamlined trains that were among the finest passenger trains in the West. Locomotives and cars were dressed in an attractive blue-and-white livery credited to Raymond Loewy and Electro-Motive's design team. MP's E3 and E6 diesels displayed custom styling with rows of porthole windows along the sides. *Robert A. Buck collection*

continued from page 108

techniques for American trains. By the mid-1930s, streamlining had set new expectations, and passenger train design was never the same afterward. Vice president of the New York Air Brake Company, L. K. Sillcox, wrote in *Railway Age* in March 1936, "Nothing less would have satisfied popular demand since a quite definite opinion has been formed as to just what appearance a high-speed train should present." Certainly, in their early days, lightweight diesel-powered articulated streamliners demonstrated lower operating costs. In February 1935 *Railway Age* reported that Burlington's *Zephyr*'s "operating cost was an average of 53 percent of the steam trains it replaced. Running maintenance and fuel costs were substantially less. The cost of fuel and lube oil was calculated at $3.88 for *Zephyr* compared with $13.77 per mile for a steam train."

At very high speeds, in excess of 100 miles per hour, aerodynamics noticeably affects train performance. The pioneering streamlined trains, such as Germany's Flying Hamburger and Burlington's *Zephyr*, pushed the limits of what could be achieved with then state-of-the-art diesel engines. While the engines offered a great power-to-weight ratio, they were not especially powerful when compared with either today's diesel or contemporary steam locomotives. Since every horsepower counted, the nominal difference offered by reducing air resistance at top speeds could be significant. To get the most out of compact powerplants to achieve sustained high-speed operation, railway designers emulated aircraft protocols by reducing weight and air resistance to the greatest extent possible. *Zephyr*'s body shape was the function of wind-tunnel tests and featured skirting and shields over the wheels to minimize air drag as much as possible.

What is high speed? How fast is it and when does it matter? Top operating speed and average speed are two different measurements. Both contribute to faster schedules. But ability to reach very high speeds compared with the need to operate at sustained moderately high speed must be considered separately. For example, in February 1935 *Railway Age* reported

DAYBREAK...

... heavy guns moving into position for action on the African Front ... planes returning from a night "bombing party" over Axis territory. And, on the home front, loaded munition trains whistling shrill warnings as they approach slumber-wrapped towns in Kansas, Massachusetts, Texas —everywhere. It is WAR—war with its toil and tears, its heroism and sacrifices.

BUT SOME DAY WILL COME ANOTHER DAWN—a sunrise that will light up a world at peace. Then trains will speed across the nation carrying ration-freed foods for America's pantries; materials for its home builders; tools and implements for its farms, factories and professions; and peace-time necessities for all!

Now we are engaged in war. America's railroads—all

vital units in the transportation army—are performing a patriotic service. Theirs is the hauling job of the nation. *And what a job they are doing*—41,000,000 tons of army freight carried in '42—11,600,000 troops transported during the first year of the war!

ROCK ISLAND'S Program of Planned Progress, begun seven years ago, is being carried on even in the midst of the war. For when the new day dawns America will demand the best in rail transportation. While today it isn't possible to buy all of the equipment and materials required, we must have the revenue now for the great backlog of purchases that some day will be released. And think of the many jobs this will make available for our boys now in uniform!

As yesterday—and today—so tomorrow ROCK ISLAND'S sole purpose is to provide the finest in transportation.

★ ★ BUY WAR BONDS AND STAMPS ★ ★

ROCK ISLAND LINES

ONE OF AMERICA'S RAILROADS — *ALL* UNITED FOR VICTORY

Rock Island was an early proponent of streamlined diesel power as featured in this World War II–era advertisement when streamlining represented a vision of the future. After the war, American railroads readily embraced the streamlined diesels to replace steam. *Solomon collection*

JAMES E. EPPENSTEIN

by John Gruber

The North Shore Line, a speedy Chicago to Milwaukee electric interurban railroad, commissioned Chicago architect James F. Eppenstein (1899–1955) to style its two four-unit articulated *Electroliner* trains, introduced in 1941.

Albert L. Arenberg, president of Luminator Company, introduced Eppenstein to North Shore officials. "Before the first meeting, my father had Jim in his office," recalled Henry Arenberg, Albert's son. "'Where's your hat?' my father asked Jim, who had this beautiful head of hair, very well done. Jim did not own a hat. Since you had to have a hat to do business with a railroad, my father went out to buy Jim a hat and together they went to the NS offices." Eppenstein got the styling contract, Arenberg the lighting contract.

The railroad and Eppenstein started out by taking a careful look at the passenger traffic. "Inasmuch as these trains are used very largely for commuting service between the various cities on the line it is natural that a very large percentage of the passengers should be women. It was therefore felt that the interiors should be unusually inviting, in order to appeal to feminine tastes," according to an article in *Mass Transportation* magazine.

"These murals reach their height in gaiety in the Tavern Car where they consist of various brightly colored animals engaged in a variety of activities—for instance, a pink elephant walking a tight rope. Here in the Tavern Car also are deep luxurious seats of a new type, designed by James Eppenstein and Associates, and not before used in transportation equipment."

Eppenstein's exterior—gray with brilliant red-orange stripes below the windows against jade green for the body of the cars—was designed "to give the impression of high speed even when the train is at rest."

Eppenstein worked at his father's factory in Elgin from 1919 to 1928. But he had always wanted to be an architect and returned to college for architectural study in the United States and Europe. He opened his architecture business in Chicago in 1934. *American Architect* featured his "impressive" office in its September 1935 issue. When admitted to the American Institute of Architects in 1939, he listed homes in Highland Park and Winnetka as examples of his work.

The *Electroliners* survive today at Orbisonia, Pennsylvania, and Union, Illinois—a tribute to their well-deserved place in the history of electric railroading.

North Shore published this colorful brochure to inform ridership about the special design and service of its new streamlined *Electroliners*. The trains were advertised as America's first "all electric trains." Among the memorable *Electroliner* experiences was the famed "Electroburgers" that were cooked on board with an electric grille. *Solomon collection*

that *Zephyr*'s regular daily run included a two-segment roundtrip journey: Lincoln to Omaha, Omaha to Kansas City, and then return. It was scheduled to make the 195-mile Omaha to Kansas City section of the run in 240 minutes, including a 6-minute stop at St. Joseph, Missouri. This was 80 minutes faster than the comparable journey by steam train. However, the *Zephyr* did this without traveling at exceptionally fast speeds. The top speed on the line was only 85 miles per hour. While its possible that engineers occasionally stepped up the pace to make up time, the point is that the train didn't require a sophisticated aerodynamic shape to run at 85 miles per hour, even with a mere 600 horsepower at its disposal.

This leads to some important questions: If Burlington could have run the train 20–30 miles per hour faster, why was it limited to 85 miles per hour? Was that really "high-speed"? And if it didn't require aerodynamic design, why go through all the extra effort? The first question is simply answered. Burlington

In the 1920s, New York Central's chief engineer Paul Kiefer pushed the six-coupled steam locomotive to its ultimate form with the design of the 4-6-4 Hudson type. To improve its performance, the highly refined locomotive type was considered for streamlining as early as 1927, yet it wasn't until 1934 when aerodynamic shrouds were first applied. The pioneer streamlined Hudson *Commodore Vanderbilt* was photographed at Collinwood, Ohio. *J. R. Quinn collection, Solomon collection*

installed this *Zephyr* on an existing line, engineered for pre-existing traffic. This was a heavy freight route, which necessarily limited the super elevation of curves and placed limitations on existing signaling. Not only would raising *Zephyr*'s speed require substantial and costly infrastructure improvements, but raising passenger train speeds without adding additional tracks would constrain the route's freight-hauling capacity. On the full 250 miles between Lincoln and Omaha, only 105 miles were equipped with directional double track.

continued on page 118

The distinctive design of General Electric's steam turbine-electric locomotives built for Union Pacific was partially the inspiration of Raymond E. Patten, an industrial designer for GE, who later worked on the Alco-GE PA and FA diesel-electric. These were intended to resemble Union Pacific's other streamlined trains. Only two of the

impressive-looking locomotives were built. Originally intended for transcontinental passenger service, they were promoted as offering twice the thermal efficiency of a conventional steam locomotive while being capable of 125 miles per hour. *Photographer unknown, John Gruber collection*

CHARLES L. EGGLESTON

by John Gruber

When Southern Pacific was planning its streamlined *Daylight*, it made the somewhat unconventional decision to keep the design work in-house, rather than commissioning a design from a professional firm, as many railroads did in the streamliner era.

SP turned to Charles L. Eggleston, an experienced draftsman in its Motive-Power department. Eggleston (1890–1971) had studied at the San Francisco Institute of Art in 1912–13, became a member of the California Society of Etchers, and exhibited at the Oakland Art Gallery in 1934.

Eggleston's work can be seen today in SP locomotive No. 4449, built in 1941 for *Daylight* service, and survives as a popular excursion locomotive based in Portland, Oregon. A postage stamp, with a Ted Rose watercolor, also recognizes the *Daylight*'s colorful design.

Eggleston, the son of a distinguished newspaper editor, was born in Syracuse, New York. The family moved to Montana where his father, Charles H. Eggleston, was associate editor of the *Anaconda Standard* for more than forty years. The son wanted to be an editorial cartoonist, but his father discouraged him from that career.

Eggleston started work for the SP before World War I. By 1924, he had designed a drumhead, or tail sign, for almost every SP passenger train. He also sketched a small, self-propelled, three-car motor train in 1933, but SP management turned it down in favor of a high-capacity, full-sized train.

Initially, SP's executive committee approved a new lightweight *Daylight* diesel train, to be built by Pullman, but soon decided to use steam instead of diesel power.

The initial route was to be its *Coast Line* between San Francisco and Los Angeles.

In late 1935, SP sent staff members east to work on design details. Eggleston spent fifteen months at a temporary office at the Pullman plant at Chicago planning the colors, insignia, and interiors for the twelve-car train. Most of the details reported here come from Richard K. Wright's book, *Daylight, Train 98-99* (1970). In those days, Wright was able to interview SP veterans who were no longer alive when research was undertaken for more recent books, such as Robert J. Church's *Southern Pacific Daylight Locomotives* (2004) and Brian Solomon's *SP Passenger Trains* (2005).

The *Daylight* trains were introduced to the public with Hollywood-style ceremonies and heavy media coverage. They made their inaugural trips from San Francisco and Los Angeles on Sunday, March 21, 1937, and were an instant success. The first day, the trains were sold out.

In October 1937, Eggleston visited the SP office in San Francisco while on vacation. He had moved permanently to the Midwest, and in 1938 he was married to Ruth Syber of Kenosha, Wisconsin. The United States Rubber Company hired him as a special representative, with an office in Chicago. He sold sponge rubber to the railroads and also continued design work for Pullman. He lived in Chicago and its northern suburbs until 1963 when he and Ruth moved to South Bend, Indiana, where Ruth's daughter and her husband lived. He continued to make etchings, and today daughter and husband proudly display them in their home. Eggleston, they say, always took pride in the *Daylight* cars—a lasting legacy to his life and artistry.

continued from page 115

The caveat to this problem answers the second question: since, *Zephyr* enabled Burlington to dramatically speed up its schedule without requiring 110-miles-per-hour operation, what was the incentive to run faster? While some railroads did routinely run trains above 100 miles per hour, including Burlington's Chicago–Minneapolis *Twin Cities Zephyr*s, the vast majority of American streamlined trains didn't operate fast enough, or maintain sustained high speed long enough to really warrant aerodynamic treatment.

So why did railroads spend the money on aerodynamic design? In the early days of streamlining,

In 1934, wind-tunnel-designed shrouds were applied to New York Central 5344 to improve its fuel efficiency. It was renamed *Commodore Vanderbilt* to honor New York Central's nineteenth-century founder. On August 20, 1936, it was captured on film westbound near Chicago. *Sirman collection*

the concept was about pushing the envelope, going faster than had ever been done before. The novelty of the aerodynamic high-speed train gripped the public's imagination. Diesels offered rapid acceleration and sustained running. However, since railroads were able to offer faster schedules by trimming unnecessary stops associated with traditional steam locomotive operation, they didn't need to regularly run at lightning fast speeds.

Later streamliners obtained operational benefit from significantly lighter passenger design owning to new lighter materials. Modern motive power, including the advancement of more powerful diesel-electrics, amply powered modern steam locomotives with roller bearings, large boiler capacity, and energy-saving devices, enabled sustained faster running.

Diesel technology advanced rapidly in the 1930s. Within just a few years General Motors' diesel engines went from a 600-horsepower to a 1,500-horsepower rating. By combining engines, single-unit twin diesels locomotives were rated at 1,800 horsepower by 1936, and by 1938 were commercially sold in pairs with a combined rating of 3,600 horsepower. Much higher

horsepower combined with new lighter passenger cars made the nominal savings afforded by true aerodynamic design irrelevant. The relative value of perfect, wind tunnel–sculpted teardrop shapes and wheel guards were negated as train lengths grew longer. What worked with a three-car *Zephyr* had little operational effect on a twelve- to twenty-car train.

Sillcox reminded readers in 1936 that the effect of new trains was "accepted by the public to the extent that all new railway equipment should be designed to afford at least a superficially streamlined appearance." For the next two decades, most road diesels, including those designed and built for freight service, embodied a streamlined appearance, regardless of the manufacturer or intended top speed.

SUMMER SCHEDULE
July 15, 1945

The New York New Haven and Hartford
RAILROAD CO.

New York New Haven and Hartford

DIESEL-ELECTRIC *between* NEW HAVEN *and* BOST

Serving NEW YORI
AND THE GREAT INDUSTRIAL STATES
MASSACHUSETT
RHODE ISLAN
CONNECTICUT

EASTERN WAR TIME

GO GREAT! ON THE INCOMPARAB

EMPIRE BUILDER
GREAT NORTHERN'S GREATEST TRAIN

GREAT NORTHERN RAILWAY

CHAPTER 4

POSTWAR STREAMLINERS

World War II was a turning point for American railroads. The war precipitated the greatest traffic surge the industry had ever experienced, and freight and passenger businesses swelled to their highest levels in history. The robust wartime economy combined with strict restrictions on commodities such as gasoline and rubber had the effect of reversing the shift toward highway and air travel. These events more effectively accomplished getting passengers back on trains than had all the flashy streamliners of the 1930s combined.

But the war affected the railroads in other ways. Following American entry into the war after events at Pearl Harbor in December 1941, the War Production Board placed limitations on industrial production to focus the use of critical materials and technology for the war effort. This curtailed railroad freedom in the selection of new locomotives and especially limited production of diesels. By 1942 the WPB had suspended most commercial passenger train construction, including locomotives and cars. There were a few exceptions, notably a fleet of Alco DL109s, built for

Left: New York Central's flagship train was the famed *20th Century Limited.* This was an exceptional train in its heyday with an all-Pullman sleeper consist—no coach passengers—that ran on an express schedule without intermediate station stops between New York's Grand Central Terminal and Chicago's LaSalle Street Station. Not only was it exclusively first class, but also required an extra fare for which passengers gladly paid. There was no better way to go. *New York Central System ad, Solomon collection*

Opposite left: This World War II–era New Haven Railroad timetable features one of the railroad's Alco DL-109 road diesels. New Haven purchased sixty of the type, which represented the bulk of production and featured a subdued variation of Kuhler's styling. These were largely assigned to passenger work during the day, while at night they hauled freight. *Solomon collection*

Opposite right: After World War II, Great Northern bought new lightweight streamlined cars for its flagship passenger train, the famed *Empire Builder* (Chicago–Seattle). Named to honor the railroad's founder, James J. Hill, *Empire Builder* was first streamlined in February 1947. This mid-1950s brochure depicts the train after domes were added. *Solomon collection*

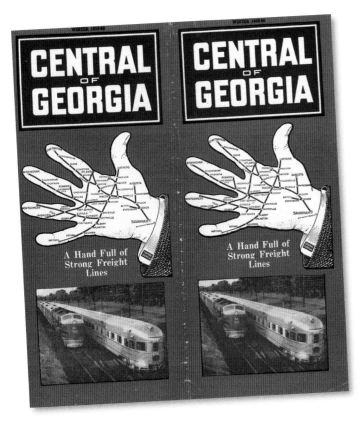

Above: Electro-Motive E7s and Budd streamlined cars grace the cover of Central of Georgia's 1959–1960 public timetable. In addition to hosting through streamliners between Chicago and Florida, such as the *City of Miami,* Central of Georgia also operated its own intra-line Atlanta–Savannah coach streamliner called *Nancy Hanks II. Solomon collection*

Right: New York Central was among railroads that initially resisted postwar dieselization and operated its finest trains with efficient modern steam power. In this view, Central's *James Whitcomb Riley* (Cincinnati–Chicago) carries a 1949 Budd-built tavern-lounge-observation at the end of a long modern stainless-steel consist led by modern steam locomotives as hinted at by the telltale exhaust smoke. It wasn't long before Central recognized the superior economics of diesels, and by the mid-1950s it had sidelined its steam power. By contrast, its Budd passenger cars survived for decades. *David Chambers, Jay Williams collection*

New Haven as dual-traffic locomotives, and some GG1 electrics for Pennsylvania Railroad. But most railroads had to cope with their existing passenger fleets for the duration of the war.

Although many railroads sought to buy diesels, War Production Board restrictions in effect from April 1942 imposed tight controls on sales and the implementation of new locomotive designs, while focusing on the types of locomotives that the major builders were allowed to sell in order to minimize difficulties with parts distribution. Copper and diesel engines were critical for the war effort, so relatively few diesel locomotives were built, and whenever possible railroads were encouraged to buy steam power. Electro-Motive was allowed limited production of road freight diesels, while the traditional steam builders were allocated

steam orders. However, while WPB required approval for specific locomotive orders and opposed implementation of major design changes, it did not specifically prohibit research and development.

As the war drew to its conclusion, locomotive and passenger car suppliers anticipated the postwar sales boom, so to remain competitive began preparing new designs during wartime production. In 1945 WPB restrictions were eased, and railroad suppliers geared up for the most intensive re-equipping of American railroading ever accomplished. Streamlining was the order of the day, and most new diesel locomotives and almost all passenger cars were advancements on the designs of the prewar period.

After World War II, New York Central re-equipped its Cincinnati–Chicago *James Whitcomb Riley* with stainless-steel Budd equipment. This view shows a 1947 Budd-built tavern-lounge-observation, a car advertised as hosting a buffet. *James Whitcomb Riley* was a premier express service on New York Central's Big Four route that departed Cincinnati in the morning and only stopped at Indianapolis and Lafayette, Indiana, and Kankakee, Illinois, for an early afternoon arrival at Chicago's Central Station. *Jay Williams collection*

Opposite top: Rock Island's Pullman-built sleeping car *Air Force Academy* was ten years old at the time of this August 1964 photo at Englewood, Illinois. This was built as part of an order for twelve cars. Unlike Budd's shot-welded stainless-steel cars, where stainless was the principle structural material, Pullman's cars used stainless steel sheathing strictly for decorative appearances. *Richard Jay Solomon*

Opposite bottom: Pennsylvania painted its passenger cars in subdued colors: Tuscan red with golden stripes bordered by black. In this September 1963 view, streamlined Pullmans on PRR's *Manhattan Limited* descend the famous Horseshoe Curve at milepost 241 near Altoona, Pennsylvania. *Richard Jay Solomon*

Overleaf: Streamliners serving the Southeast benefited from through operation over Pennsylvania Railroad north of Washington, DC to Baltimore, Philadelphia, and New York City. In the early 1960s, a PRR GG1 streamlined electric leads Seaboard Air Line's *Silver Meteor* with Budd lightweight cars southward over the Raritan River at New Brunswick, New Jersey. By 1949, Seaboard was offering three streamliners daily between New York City and Southeastern destinations. *Richard Jay Solomon*

General Motors Diesels

In the years leading up to the war, General Motors Electro-Motive Corporation (renamed Electro-Motive Division in 1940) had successfully demonstrated the capabilities of diesel-electric motive power in all types of heavy service. Its clever "automotivization" of the locomotive business combined compact high-output, naval-style diesel engines with rugged electrical components refined for railroad service, while packaging the engines in a sexy streamlined style derived and adapted from automobile and truck designs of the day. EMC's introduction of the model FT in 1939 changed how railroads viewed motive power. This model for the first time showed that a diesel could match and exceed the output of big steam.

In its original configuration, the FT was built as a four-unit 5,400-horsepower locomotive geared for maximum 75-miles-per-hour operation. Individually, each unit was rated at 1,350 horsepower. GM's choice *continued on page 128*

Compared with passenger streamliners that were introduced with great fanfare and accompanied by detailed articles in the trade press, Electro-Motive's FT made a stealthy debut in late 1939 but was taken very seriously by railroad management. Electro-Motive demonstrator set No. 103 proved its capabilities as a heavy freight hauler while traveling more than 83,000 miles on 20 Class I railroads across thirty-five states. It is pictured on its demonstration run about 1940. By the end of the decade most North American railroads had bought F-units for freight service. *Photographer unknown, Solomon collection*

---

continued from page 124

of output was significant. Only the very largest steam locomotives could conceivably out pull a four-unit FT. But while big steam was limited to the heaviest built lines, the FT was design to operate almost anywhere, giving diesels greater versatility (and four-unit sets could be divided into two 2,700-horsepower locomotives), as well as greater availability, better thermal efficiency, better economy, and overall lower cost of operation.

During World War II, General Motors' diesels demonstrated exceptional service, while facilitating the manufacturer to further refine and improve its technology, which allowed it to introduce even better diesels after the war. GM locomotives were the face of dieselization, and in those days appearance mattered. Not only was GM the largest and most successful purveyor of diesels, but it also designed paint schemes,

helped railroads prepare for dieselization, and set the new standards and patterns for locomotive type emulated by its competition.

Today, it might seem strange that railroads would invest vast sums for streamlined locomotives that would largely toil out of the public view. But, GM's FT was an outgrowth of the successful passenger E-unit design, and the essential technology refined for the E-unit had been adapted and rearranged for the FT. In addition to similar mechanical and electric systems, the two types shared the same essential streamlined carbody. Also, the FT was intended to serve as its own best advertisement, so it was important that it looked progressive, modern, colorful, clean and, of course, streamlined. The FT was designed to present a distinct contrast to awkwardly proportioned steam locomotives that had ruled the rails for a century. By 1945 it was expected that road diesels would be colorful streamlined machines.

The face of GM's postwar diesels was the "bulldog nose" introduced with the FT, and which was a design

continued on page 133

Opposite: Streamlined car body style construction remained standard for most American road-diesels from the late-1930s until the mid-1950s. Electro-Motive's model FT was the first of its F-units. Built from 1939 to 1945, this model can easily be distinguished from postwar Fs by its row of four evenly spaced porthole windows on each side of the locomotive. *Solomon collection*

Locomotive "No. 1" which puffed its way across the dales of mid-Wisconsin in 1851 was one of the trail blazers for the present magnificent transcontinental system of the Milwaukee Road.

Movement of vital war freight was speeded and tonnage increased when the Milwaukee Railroad installed General Motors Diesel Locomotives on the 225-mile mountain zone between Avery, Idaho, and Othello, Washington.

PATTERN FOR FINER TRANSPORTATION

WRITTEN into the grueling war job the railroads of America are doing, is the story of this mighty titan of the rails. This is the General Motors Diesel Locomotive. It is displaying the unusual stamina, speed and willingness to work ceaselessly which these urgent times demand. And with such tireless, low-cost, swift service these GM Diesel Locomotives are providing a pattern for finer transportation in the greater days to come.

★
KEEP
AMERICA
STRONG
BUY MORE
WAR BONDS
★

GM
GENERAL MOTORS
DIESEL POWER

LOCOMOTIVES............*ELECTRO-MOTIVE DIVISION*, La Grange, Ill.

ENGINES.....150 to 2000 H.P.....*CLEVELAND DIESEL ENGINE DIVISION*, Cleveland 11, Ohio

ENGINES........15 to 250 H.P........*DETROIT DIESEL ENGINE DIVISION*, Detroit 23, Mich.

On May 23, 1946, Rock Island's *Rocky Mountain Rocket* works west of Joliet, Illinois. Rock Island had peculiar locomotive requirements for this train, which was split at Limon, Colorado, with separate sections destined for Denver and Colorado Springs. To keep the number of locomotives assigned to the train to a minimum, the trailing

locomotive was a specially designed E-unit model variant designated an AB6, which had a flat-front similar to that of a B-unit but featured a fully operational cab. West of Limon this would lead the Colorado Springs section, while the Denver section continued on behind the streamlined cab. *John E. Pickett collection*

For Fast, Dependable Freight Deliveries

Freights high-balling down the right-of-way at almost passenger speeds! Your merchandise at destination many precious hours ahead of time! Fast, courteous, trouble-free handling of all your transportation needs to, from, and through the main traffic lane of the booming Southwest!

All these are yours with the precision rail transportation now offered by the Southwest's home-town railroad. Five crack Katy Freights, operating on stepped-up daily schedules, afford dependable, on-time service between St. Louis, Kansas City and important points in Missouri, Kansas, Oklahoma and Texas, with extensive connecting service at terminals.

Free Pick-Up and Delivery of L.C.L. Freight

Delivery **from** any point in the U. S. **to** any major on-line city . . . Pick up **from** any on-line city **to** any point in the U. S.

Katy Truck

CO-ORDINATED FREIGHT SERVICE TO KANSAS POINTS

One-day deliveries from St. Louis or Kansas City to Parsons, Fort Scott, Paola, Iola, Moran, Erie, Coffeyville, Chetopa, Oswego. One day from Kansas City,

second morning from St. Louis to Junction City, Council Grove, Emporia, Burlington, Humbolt, Chanute and intermediate points.

Streamlined diesels, which had been but a novelty before World War II, became the norm after the war. Regardless of whether they were used for express passenger service or heavy freight, most new road locomotives were built with streamlined car bodies. The most common types were Electro-Motive's F-units, built by the thousands in the 1940s and early 1950s. In this 1946 advertisement, Katy Line's Electro-Motive F3s convey speed and reliability for the company's fast freight services. *Solomon collection*

A stylized Pennsylvania Railroad E8A graces the cover of the railroad's ticket sheath (E8As were built from 1949–55). PRR was America's largest passenger railroad. While the railroad resisted dieselization until after World War II, and initially operated one of the most diverse rosters of passenger diesels, it was ultimately the largest buyer of Electro-Motive E-units, which included 74 E8As. *Solomon collection*

continued from page 128

refinement over the steeply slanted front of prewar E-units. This nose was more than just good looks, it was a heavily reinforced buffer designed to protect crews in the event of a collision while giving them a superior forward view. The nose section was constructed from four separate sheets of pressed 12-gauge steel combined with a cylindrical headlight housing welded to the locomotive carbody frame. Reinforced underframing provided additional structural support. The compound curves connecting sheet steel and headlight housing were made from automotive bonding putty. (The style, slope and angle of windshields were similar to those featured on late-1930s Buick automobiles.) Inside the cab the handles used to "roll down" windows were virtually identical to those in GM's automobiles.

Engineers who worked the early Pullman/Electro-Motive streamliners played key rolls in the design of the F-unit. Notably, Martin Blomberg, who had devised structural designs for Union Pacific's M-10000 and other early trains and participated closely in development of the E-unit, also designed the four-wheel "Blomberg" truck for the FT—a type that remained the standard wheel-set for most four-axle Electro-Motive diesels into the 1990s.

Electro-Motive's improved F-unit models were by far the best-selling type after the war. Its F3 model, built from 1945 to 1949, featured a slightly longer carbody than FT and introduced a host of technical improvements that made it more powerful, more

Delaware, Lackawanna & Western displayed this new FT set at Binghamton, New York, on June 23, 1945. An estimated 12,000 people stopped by to inspect the new engines. Like the earlier model E-units, Electro-Motive's Model FT used a streamlined car-body that was integral to the structure of the locomotive. *Robert A. Buck collection*

versatile, and a vastly more reliable locomotive. Similar technological advancements were applied to Electro-Motive's postwar E-units, beginning with its E7, also introduced in 1945.

The streamlined Fs were assigned to every kind of road service from hauling Maine potatoes to Minnesota iron ore, and working local, commuter, and express passenger trains, singularly and in multiple. Over the twenty-one-year production run ending in 1960, more than 7,600 individual F-units had been sold in North America (including the prewar and wartime FT units). This streamliner operated on all but a handful of railroads and was universally recognized as the American diesel locomotive. Today, when recalling the streamlined era, it is typically an image of a bulldog nose on an E- or F-unit that comes to mind.

Diesel Competition

In the early days of American dieselization, Alco led the way before General Motors eclipsed it. During World War II, although its factories were geared toward steam locomotive production, Alco anticipated the postwar demand for diesels. Beginning in 1940,

RAYMOND E. PATTEN

by John Gruber

An industrial designer who specialized in appliances helped shape the distinctive appearance of Alco and General Electric locomotives. Raymond E. Patten's best-known railroad designs are for the PA (passenger) and FA (freight) diesel locomotives in 1946. Patten (1897–1948), director of GE's Appearance Design Division of the Appliance and Merchandising department in Bridgeport, Connecticut, also influenced the designs for electric and industrial locomotives and the ill-fated Union Pacific steam-turbine electric. From 1940 to 1953 Alco and GE jointly marketed large road locomotives.

Alco-GE distributed a six-page article Patten prepared. The goal, he said, was: "A locomotive so distinctive and so powerful looking that it actually helps the railroads sell their services to passengers and shippers."

From rough pencil sketches of the exterior, executives selected the basic design. The fluted headlight, "devised to obtain product identity and serve as a focal point," was changed to meet ICC regulations. The modifications throughout the design process are reflected in the advertising. Melbourne Brindle's painting for the August 1946 GE calendar and other early illustrations, for example, show the headlight grille before it was moved higher on the nose of the locomotive. A *Trains* magazine cover, September 1946, features an early version of the PA.

Patten attended the Massachusetts Institute of Technology and started his career with the Hume Body Corporation, Boston, and continued custom body designs with the Dayton Wright Company. He spent five years with the Packard Motor Car Commune of Detroit. He joined the Edison GE Company in Chicago in 1928. When moving to Bridgeport in 1934, he was the only person in the Appliance Design department. Under his leadership, the department grew to fifty by 1946, broadening its tasks to include packaging and the inside and outside of dealer stores.

Although virtually unknown today, Patten was a prominent designer in the 1940s. He was one of fifteen founding members of the Society of Industrial Designers, organized in February 1944.

Alco and General Electric worked jointly designing and marketing large road locomotives with GE supplying electrical components.

In September 1945, Alco-GE finished an experimental A-B-A road-diesel with Otto Kuhler styling that appeared like a compressed variation of the prewar DL109. Painted black, it came to be known as "Black Maria" (pronounced with a hard *I*). Testing concluded in November 1946, and the experimental was cut up in 1947.

By that time, Alco had introduced freight and passenger diesels using distinctive carbodies. GE's Raymond E. Patten (see sidebar) was responsible for the shape and style of Alco and General Electric's carbody locomotives in the postwar years. Appearances were important and Patten's designs were intended to help distinguish the Alco-GE diesels from those produced by General Motors.

Alco-GE's FA/FB was a four-axle type, initially identified in advertising and company literature as simply the "Alco-G.E. 1,500 Diesel-Electric Road Freight Locomotive." This was Alco's equivalent to the FT. The first FA's were built for Gulf, Mobile & Ohio in 1946. In the 1950s, Alco's Canadian affiliate, Montreal Locomotive Works, built passenger variations designated as models FPA-2/FPA-4.

Alco-GE's PA/PB postwar passenger locomotive replaced its older Otto Kuhler–styled DL109 type. Although it shared a family appearance with the FA models, the PA's longer frame provided more appealing proportions for Patten's characteristic style. Its 6-foot-long "nose" section, longer body (65 feet. 8 inches over couplers), and three-axle trucks gave the locomotive a distinctive pleasing appearance that has been considered one of the best-looking American locomotives.

Above: The Alco PA passenger diesel made its mark with railway enthusiasts, many of whom consider it the finest-looking streamlined diesel ever built. In July 1956, New Haven Railroad PAs led an excursion eastbound near the west end of the normally freight-only Poughkeepsie Bridge that spans New York's Hudson River. *Jim Shaughnessy*

Left: Alco's FA/FB freight diesels and its PA passenger diesels shared similar styling. On August 20, 1965, Lehigh Valley FA/FBs lead an eastward freight at Sayre, Pennsylvania. *Jim Shaughnessy*

TWO-UNIT PERMANENTLY COUPLED
DIESEL-ELECTRIC LOCOMOTIVE

For fast, through passenger service. Wheel
arrangement: 4-8-8-4 each unit. Pennsylvania
Class BP-1.

Coupled Length	183 feet, 0 inches
Driving Wheel Diameter	42 inches
Weight on Driving Wheels	818,000 pounds
Total Weight in Working Order	1,187,420 pounds
Starting Tractive Force	204,500 pounds
Horsepower	6,000

In 1947 and 1948 Pennsylvania Railroad bought twenty-four big Baldwin model DR-12-8-3000s for passenger service. The locomotives were better known as "Centipedes" and were relegated to freight work in later years. *Solomon collection*

Baldwin's Streamlined Diesels

Since the nineteenth century, Philadelphia-based Baldwin Locomotive Works had been America's foremost steam locomotive manufacturer. While it was among the earliest to experiment with diesel power, and began selling diesel switchers in the 1930s, it delayed development of road diesels until after World War II. This late entry into the diesel market combined with a variety of technological problems didn't aid Baldwin's sales of road diesels. They were reported to have suffered from poor reliability compared with those built by Electro-Motive and Alco. Relatively few were sold and so were less common on American rails. Yet Baldwin produced some of the most interesting streamlined diesels of the postwar period.

Baldwin began engineering streamlined road diesels during World War II, but its initial designs followed a divergent approach from that of other builders by emulating modern steam and electric locomotive practice: it aimed to build a single, very powerful unit that could match the output of modern steam and electrics. It settled on the 2-D+D-2-wheel arrangement that was an outgrowth of Baldwin and Westinghouse's heavy electric designs. A massive 6,000-horsepower prototype was built during the war but deemed a failure. However in 1945, Seaboard Air Line expressed interest in the 2-D+D-2-wheel arrangement, so Baldwin

Opposite: In 1950, Fairbanks-Morse introduced its new Consolidation line (commonly known as "C-Liners"). Although similar in appearance to the earlier "Erie-built" diesels, these streamlined F-M diesels featured a more refined exterior design. They were available in eleven different configurations ranging from 1,600 to 2,400 horsepower per unit, powered by F-M's powerful opposed-piston engines. However, they were relatively rare compared with General Motors E- and F-units. *Solomon collection*

A NEW PAGE

IN CANADIAN RAILROAD HISTORY

Arrival of the first Fairbanks-Morse Consolidation Locomotive at Kingston signalled the start of a new page in Canadian railroad history.

New in design . . . new in performance . . . Consolidation Locomotives powered by Fairbanks-Morse Opposed-Piston Diesel Engines have already established new standards of efficiency, economy and dependable service. Fairbanks, Morse & Co., Chicago 5, Illinois.

Opposed-Piston Powered Consolidation Locomotives are made in Canada by the Canadian Locomotive Co., Ltd.

 FAIRBANKS-MORSE,
a name worth remembering when you want the best

DIESEL LOCOMOTIVES AND ENGINES • ELECTRICAL MACHINERY • PUMPS • SCALES
HOME WATER SERVICE EQUIPMENT • RAIL CARS • FARM MACHINERY • MAGNETOS

redesigned its road diesel from the wheels up. This featured a new carbody style with the so-called "baby face" cab—a streamlined front end that looked remarkably similar to Electro-Motive's "bulldog nose," albeit with a different expression. In advertising, Baldwin boasted: "World's most powerful single-unit, diesel-electric [is] another example of Baldwin pioneering in the field of railway motive power." Known technically as model DR-12-8-3000 or DR-12-8-1500/2, it was more commonly known as the "Baldwin Centipede." Only Seaboard, Pennsylvania Railroad, and National Railways of Mexico bought the type.

Beginning in 1944, Baldwin also developed a road passenger diesel model essentially patterned on Electro-Motive's E-unit. Postwar versions were streamlined with the baby face cab, but very few were sold. A variation for Central Railroad of New Jersey was a Janus-like double-ender, with cabs at both ends. Pennsylvania Railroad bought a distinctive streamlined variation with styling characteristics similar to the T1 *Duplex* steam engine, known colloquially as the "Shark Nose." This design was ultimately applied to several locomotive models, including four-axle freight diesels sold to Pennsylvania, Baltimore & Ohio, and New York Central. By the mid-1950s sales hit modern lows as Electro-Motive had sewn up most of the market and dieselization was nearing completion. So in 1956, Baldwin effectively ended diesel production except for a few hydraulic transmission, lightweight power cars for Pullman's Train-X (see Chapter 5).

Fairbanks-Morse

Fairbanks-Morse was a railroad supply and engine manufacturing company that by 1940 had become the second-largest diesel engine builder in the United States. In the 1930s, it supplied engines for some semi-streamlined railcars for Southern Railway and during World War II provided large numbers of engines for submarines and other military applications. As wartime demand for its successful opposed-piston diesel engine waned it looked to capitalize on the locomotive market, and in mid-1944 it entered the heavy domestic locomotive business. Although initially limited by the War Production Board to building switchers, after the war it introduced a locomotive line complete with large streamlined road diesels comparable to those offered by other builders.

Pennsylvania Railroad's fifty production T1s, plus the two prototypes, made this class one of the most numerous types of streamlined steam in the United States. There were several varieties of Loewy styling, with later locomotives more conservatively styled than the prototypes. This new engine was photographed at Englewood, Illinois, on May 26, 1946; it was among the early production locomotives and featured a row of portholes on the pilot. *Courtesy of J.R. Quinn, Solomon collection*

While F-M's primary factory was at Beloit, Wisconsin, its first streamlined carbody road diesels, built between 1945 and 1949, used bodies erected under contract by General Electric at Erie, Pennsylvania. These were forever known as "Erie-builts" to railroaders and enthusiasts—impressive-looking machines rated at 2,000 horsepower and powered by large ten-cylinder opposed-piston engines. The front ends resembled that of a ship's prow, while

the proportions of the carbody shared similarities with the GE-Alco PA.

In 1950, F-M introduced its much-improved Consolidation line diesels (popularly known as "C-Liners") that featured streamlined carbodies similar to the Erie-built units in general appearance but with a shorter nose section and a more refined exterior design. The Canadian Locomotive Company at Kingston, Ontario, built these at Beloit for the domestic market and under license for Canadian National and Canadian Pacific. Road-switcher types dominated F-M's later production. In the early 1960s, it withdrew from the locomotive market.

Last Rally for Steam

In 1939 the diesel was still a novelty, just beginning to prove its capabilities. By 1949 orders for new steam locomotives had all but finished, and diesels were on their way to total supremacy. Nevertheless, after the war a few large railroads, including Chesapeake & Ohio; Duluth, Missabe & Iron Range; New York Central, Norfolk & Western; and Pennsylvania, continued to buy modern and extraordinarily powerful steam locomotives for a few more years.

Pennsylvania took the most unusual approach, opting to refine the nonstandard *Duplex* type that it had introduced before the war with its Loewy-styled S1, a futuristic streamlined leviathan. The concept behind the *Duplex* was that it had a divided drive on a rigid frame using two complete sets of running gear; this was intended to reduce the length of the piston thrusts so as to lessen the weight of drive rods and other reciprocating gear, and thus minimize the effects of damaging pounding forces caused by reciprocating parts.

During World War II, PRR's Juniata shops built a pair of highly engineered class T1 *Duplex* passenger
continued on page 144

OLIVE W. DENNIS

by John Gruber

Olive W. Dennis (1885–1957), a research engineer for the Baltimore & Ohio, designed both a streamlined train and a popular set of railroad dining car china.

The *Cincinnatian*, a train that initially ran between Baltimore and Cincinnati, debuted January 19, 1947. B&O crafted the equipment in its Mount Clare shops, refitting older Pacific locomotives and remodeling older cars inside and out to specifications provided by Dennis. The well-spaced, individual reclining seats were her idea; so were interior walls of "glass-smooth marlite plastic," which proved very easy to clean; restroom floors of ceramic tile; water bottles with sanitary tops; harmonized, decorative schemes that varied from car to car; and murals at the end of coaches, using scenes selected largely by her.

For the china, Dennis drew upon "the outstanding features of the Baltimore and Ohio's history and to the most representative scenic points along its lines." The borders around the edges of the central images depict the sequence of development of B&O engines and passenger equipment, beginning with a horse-drawn car. Although widely known today as B&O blue china in the centennial or centenary series, it was referred to by the company as its Colonial pattern when introduced and displayed in the 1927 Fair of the Iron Horse that celebrated the road's 100th birthday. Initially, it was used almost exclusively on B&O's fleet of *Colonial*-style dining cars. Buoyed by its popularity with travelers, its use was eventually expanded to nearly all B&O diners, ending with the discontinuance of the *Capitol Limited* on May 1, 1971. Since then, it has periodically been manufactured and sold to the public through the B&O Railroad Museum in Baltimore.

Dennis was the first woman member of the National Railway Engineering Association, which gave her a standing ovation for an address she delivered in 1929. She graduated with a Phi Beta Kappa key in 1908 from Goucher College, then a Methodist college for women in downtown Baltimore, having majored in mathematics and science. She worked as a teacher and continued her education in math, astronomy, piano, voice, physical education, and surveying. She enrolled in Cornell's civil

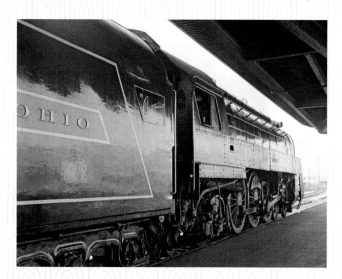

After World War II, Olive Dennis styled four Baltimore & Ohio 4-6-2 Pacifics for special service on the *Cincinnatian*. In September 1952, locomotive 5301 is photographed at Cincinnati Union Station—a glorious art deco-styled terminal that was a postwar mecca for streamlined steam. *Wallace A. Abbey, courtesy of the Center for Railroad Photography & Art, www.railphoto-art.org*

Baltimore & Ohio took a homegrown approach with its *Cincinnatian*, preferring custom-designed streamlined steam and rebuilt heavyweight cars instead of commercially built diesels and lightweight cars. In this view, B&O's class P7d Pacific 5301 leads the *Cincinnatian* (Baltimore–Cincinnati), which operated on a 12-hour 30-minute daily schedule via Grafton, West Virginia. *Photographer unknown, Solomon collection*

One of four
streamlined
Baltimore & Ohio
4-6-2s with shrouds
styled by Olive
Dennis in 1946
for service on
the *Cincinnatian*.
*Photographer
unknown,
Solomon collection*

engineering program in 1919 and finished in 1920 at the top of her class. She was only the second woman to graduate from Cornell's engineering program. Daniel Willard, B&O president from 1910 to 1940, hired Dennis to work as a draftsman in the railroad's Bridge and Engineering department. Willard then appointed her as engineer of service.

In addition, she was named Mountain Sheep Woman by Blackfoot Indians at the Fair of the Iron Horse. In connection with the fair, she designed the costumes for participants in the pageants and other theatrical endeavors. In 1925 she formed the B&O's Women's Music Club.

A year before Dennis retired from the B&O on February 28, 1951, she produced a two-volume supplementary arithmetic textbook, *Railroad 'Rithmetic*, intended to "add zest to the working out of arithmetic problems that seem dull when divorced from reality."

Norfolk & Western's streamlined J-Class 601 stands majestically at Cincinnati Union Station in September 1952. N&W remained loyal to steam longer than any other major railroad in the United States. While most railroads began dieselization after World War II, N&W continued to build new steam until the early 1950s and wasn't

completely dieselized until 1960. Among its elegant streamlined passenger trains were *The Powhatan Arrow* and *The Pocahontas*, both connecting Norfolk, Virginia, with Cincinnati via Roanoke. *Wallace A. Abbey, courtesy of the Center for Railroad Photography & Art, www.railphoto-art.org*

continued from page 139

prototypes that used the more conservative 4-4-4-4-wheel arrangement and had more practical proportions than S1. These featured distinctive Loewy styling with an impressive nautical appearance. Their design parameters were intended to equal the performance of the GG1 electric and thus allow the locomotive to haul up to 1,000 trailing tons at up to 100 miles per hour over the 713-mile run between Harrisburg, Pennsylvania, (at the western end of PRR's electrified zone) and Chicago with just a single midtrip stop for coal.

Following months of extensive testing, PRR's engineers were satisfied they had produced a locomotive worthy of high-speed long haul service that could begin to replace the famed K4s Pacifics in long-distance service. Following the war PRR ordered 50 T1s for passenger service. It was the largest order for streamlined steam locomotives in the United States. In addition, PRR also built a semi-streamlined freight *Duplex* prototype class Q1, followed by a similar post-war fleet of enormously powerful Q2 *Duplexes*. All suffered from mechanical problems. This added to already high maintenance costs that doomed them to short service lives. It was a final fleeting gasp at pushing the limits of steam to new levels. Yet, the T1s remain one of the most interesting types of American

Looks can be deceiving: at first glance, this Norfolk & Western streamlined steam locomotive might be mistaken for one of its famous J-class 4-8-4s. In fact, this is one of its Baldwin-built Class K2A 4-8-2 *Mountain* types N&W overhauled after World War II. In addition to shrouds, the old locomotives were equipped with roller bearings and modern appliances to improve efficiency. N&W *Mountain* type No. 130 arrives at Roanoke, Virginia, leading a train of prewar heavyweight cars from Hagerstown, Maryland. *Jay Williams collection*

design, N&W's engineers aimed to refine an established type into a true thoroughbred locomotive.

In the late-1930s, Norfolk & Western recognized its need for a fast, modern locomotive, capable of hauling long trains at speed on level track while able to work its mountain grades without assistance and having sufficient mechanical reliability to work the length of the railroad without need for major servicing en route. Streamlining was designed in the mode of the time to match the good looks of diesels, without disguising the machinery: there would be no question that N&W's premier passenger engine of the time would be a steam locomotive.

The first five J-class locomotives, beginning with engine 600, were built in late 1941 and early 1942, just as America was entering World War II. Interestingly, the bullet-nose shape of the J's shrouds embodied a stylistic similarity with that applied to steam locomotives designed for New York Central's *Empire State Express*, which debuted at the same time. N&W chose classic sedate colors, painting the body of the locomotive glossy black with a distinct Tuscan red side band bordered with gold striping. *Railway Age* described the J's styling in June 2, 1945, "The shrouding effects a straight line flush with the top of the cab and conceals the stack, bell, whistle, low water alarm, sand boxes, dome, turrets and feed-water heater." In other words, the shrouding hid from sight all the external protrusions that typically cluttered the appearance of an American locomotive boiler.

Although handsome, N&W's J-class earned their reputation on performance rather than appearances. By any measure these were exceptional machines. Key to its performance was an amply sized boiler, designed for sustained power and speed. N&W's engineers employed lightweight reciprocating parts made possible by the latest steel alloys, with extensive application of roller bearings combined with intensive mechanical

streamlined steam, and they inspired a class of similarly styled locomotives in Australia.

Perhaps the most successful, if not the most numerous, example of streamlined steam power was Norfolk & Western's famous J-Class 4-8-4s. These elegant, powerful machines have stirred the imagination of railway observers for generations. N&W, like PRR, built its own locomotives, which makes a comparison between PRR's T1 with the J-Class appropriate. Both were examples of late-era steam development. The two types were also variations of four-coupled steam, both were streamlined, and both were capable of great power and speed. Where PRR opted for unconventional

The silhouette of San Francisco's Golden Gate Bridge and neon lettering were classic icons for the *California Zephyr*. The advertisement set the tone for the journey: every passenger boarding the train in the gloom of Chicago Union Station would pass this glowing vision of the West on the illuminated neon sign on the observation car. *Brian Solomon*

lubrication systems that applied oil or grease to 336 individual points of friction to maximize the locomotive's potential.

In service, the Js proved exceptionally capable and were among the most utilized locomotives in America. *Railway Age* pointed out that one of the class racked up 3,368.3 miles in a week, while most of the class frequently hit 15,000 miles a month. This utilization was vastly superior to most American engines, many of which worked little more than 100 miles a day. The Js were routinely assigned to work the length of N&W's mainline, 676.6 miles between Norfolk, Virginia, and Cincinnati, Ohio.

Although an immediate success, from the time of delivery the first five Js were taxed to their maximum to meet the swell of wartime passenger traffic. N&W wanted more passenger engines, but the War Production Board's moratorium on building new passenger steam resulted in N&W building six nonstreamlined Js, notionally as freight locomotives, and without all the trappings of the first five. *Railway Age* noted in 1945 that the Js were "exclusively passenger power." After the war, N&W applied streamlining to the ugly sisters, as well as to many of its older 4-8-2 *Mountain* types.

Significantly, in 1950 N&W's Roanoke Shops built three more J class 4-8-4s, Nos. 611 to 613. By this time America's three large commercial steam builders had ceased domestic steam production. So these Js earned their place as the last new passenger steam built in the United States, as well as the last new streamlined

steam locomotives, although Roanoke Shops continued building freight steam for a few more years. It's interesting to note that by the time these final Js were built, many of the earliest American streamlined steam locomotives had lost their shrouds.

Even N&W couldn't hold back the tide of dieselization indefinitely, and by the late-1950s, diesels were working alongside steam on the road. Sadly, the J-Class was among the first to be knocked off premier runs; by 1957 borrowed Atlantic Coast Line E-units were working some of N&W's long-distance trains. Although most of the J-Class was scrapped, locomotive No. 611 was preserved. In 1982, it was restored to service, and for a dozen years worked in Norfolk Southern excursion service looking very much the way it had in its heyday. As of 2014, it was undergoing a second restoration, and soon this popular machine will be under steam again.

Concept Trains and Dome Cars

American railroads' postwar optimism inspired new equipment designs and fueled concept trains. Where the prewar streamliners focused on speeding up schedules and reducing operating and maintenance costs, while inspiring passenger confidence with new and innovative styling, postwar streamliners were aimed more at improving passenger comfort and making the most of the rail-travel experience.

General Motors, which had been the driving force of the 1930s streamlined trains, remained at the forefront. Rather than sit back and let outside forces direct industry trends, GM took an active role, not only in promoting and selling diesel locomotives, but also in continued promotion of streamlined train design. Key was its dome car innovation.

The basic idea for an elevated passenger platform to take in scenic vistas wasn't new. Canadian Pacific had experimented with a primitive version of this concept decades earlier. The inspiration for the streamlined "Astra Dome" as it was originally known, is credited to GM's Cyrus R. Osborn, who from 1943 served as a vice president of Electro-Motive. The story goes that a cab ride on the Rio Grande FT in the Colorado Rockies gave Osborn the idea that a spectacular forward view could benefit passenger travel. By 1945, GM had drafted dome car designs in planning the prototype lightweight, streamlined, dome-liner billed as the *Train of Tomorrow*.

"I know why

the California Zephyr is the most talked-about train in the country!"

"Why do I know? Because I'm a Zephyrette (the name's Nellie O'Grady) and I've made over a hundred round-trips aboard this Vista-Dome streamliner. As the California Zephyr's official 'hostess', I naturally have a chance to chat with just about every passenger on every trip. And believe me, they do talk about this wonderful train!"

"Like my dinner? I like every meal on the Zephyr! Thank goodness my wife isn't here to count the calories when the Steward comes around with one of those wonderful menus!"

"Any good shots? If not, it's my own fault! What could be more scenic than the Rockies and Feather River Canyon! No wonder this train was picked to star in 'Cinerama Holiday'!"

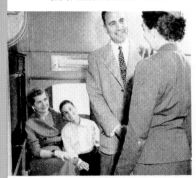

"Having fun? You bet we are! This is the first time the whole family has made the trip. Got lots of room in this Bedroom Suite, and we're saving money by using Family Fares."

"Enjoying myself? It's the most fun I've ever had on a trip to the Coast! There's so much to do and see...all those Vista-Domes, Lounge Cars, and so on. And you meet such nice people!"

"Comfortable? Young lady, I'm always comfortable when I travel in these Vista-Dome Chair Coaches. Fact is, I'd like to have this reclining chair in my living room at home!"

"Signal green? Sure it is! Up here in the Vista-Dome I can see way ahead just like the engineer does. And right after we left Moffat Tunnel I saw a whole herd of deer right down near the track!"

THE VISTA-DOME *California Zephyr*

The most popular train between Chicago and Oakland - San Francisco
via Denver and Salt Lake City

WESTERN PACIFIC

Include Southern California via San Francisco without additional rail fare • PULLMANS • CHAIR CARS

Write to Jos. G. Wheeler, Dept. NG-I, Western Pacific, 526 Mission St., San Francisco 5, for 16-page illustrated California Zephyr booklet.

Introduced in 1949, the *California Zephyr* epitomized the postwar streamliners with its prolific application of Budd *Vista Domes* and Electro-Motive diesel power. It also arguably featured the most scenic transcontinental route, which included a spectacular ascent of the Colorado Front Range, passage through Glenwood Canyon, California's rugged Feather River Canyon, and finally over Altamont Pass on the final leg of its westward journey. *Solomon collection*

In the early 1950s, Denver Union Station was a mecca for western streamliners. This February 1953 view luxuriates in shot-welded stainless steel with a trailing view of the *California Zephyr* and its characteristic Budd *Vista Domes*. The *Zephyr* operated over Burlington from Chicago, with Denver & Rio Grande Western taking it to Salt Lake City where it was handed over to Western Pacific for its final leg to the West Coast. *Wallace A. Abbey, courtesy of the Center for Railroad Photography & Art, www.railphoto-art.org*

Burlington again played a high-profile role. In 1945, it took the initiative and, working from GM's concept, its Aurora, Illinois, shops reworked a Budd stainless-steel coach into its own glass-top prototype named *Silver Dome*. From the beginning this was envisioned as a means of promoting long-distance train travel in the West. *Railway Age* described the car in November 17, 1945, noting that such cars would be "most advantageous" when assigned to trains passing scenic countryside.

Of the myriad innovative nonrevenue car designs explored after the war, the dome was the only one that attracted widespread interest. Burlington placed an order with Budd for forty similar "Vistadomes," which were delivered in 1947. They were initially assigned to the ever-popular *Twin Cities Zephyr* run so that passengers could soak in the scenic splendor of the Mississippi Valley, "where nature smiles—three hundred miles." Burlington was not only the first, but also one of the largest operators of domes. The concept was widely adopted for luxury streamlined trains, primarily among western railroads that enjoyed better vertical clearances and tended to encourage long-distance travel as a means of experiencing the scenery.

In the meantime, General Motors design teams perfected dome design for its *Train of Tomorrow*, which it had begun planning as early as 1944. This was a joint effort between various GM divisions, including Electro-Motive, and Pullman-Standard, which was contracted to build the train in 1947. GM made

it clear that although it designed the train, the project was strictly intended as an innovation showcase, and that the automotive manufacturer had no interest in building its own passenger trains. Each of the four *Astra Domes* featured a different layout representing futuristic variations on standard car types—coach, diner, sleeper, and observation lounge—but embodied design features and arrangements that deviated from conventional practices. The domes had a comparatively low profile so that they could operate over most mainlines, even those with more restrictive

continued on page 152

Union Pacific bought the four uniquely designed, Pullman-built *Astra Domes* designed by General Motors for its *Train of Tomorrow* postwar concept train. Each of the four cars featured different layouts and functions. There was a coach, sleeping car, dining car, and a round-end observation lounge. UP assigned equipment to its nameless train 458 working the Seattle–Portland run, seen in August 1953 departing Seattle. *Robert A. Buck*

On the
Vista-Dome

NORTH COAST LIMITED...

Stewardess-Nurse Service

All-Room Slumbercoaches

Vista-Dome Sleepers

Vista-Dome Coaches

Exciting Traveller's Rest
Buffet-Lounge

PASSENGER TRAIN
SCHEDULES

Time Folder issued May 28, 1961

Time Folder issued May 28, 1961

Northern Pacific's streamlined *North Coast Limited* was a queen among passenger trains. The railroad invested in streamlined equipment in 1946, and the new trainsets entered service a year later. NP augmented its transcontinental service with *Vista Domes* in the 1950s. *North Coast Limited* traveled Burlington's lines between Chicago and the Twin Cities, then over the length of Northern Pacific's mainline to Seattle with a section to Portland. *Solomon collection*

Opposite: General Motors conceived of its *Train of Tomorrow* as an advanced train to display a variety of innovative new features including the elevated *Astra Dome*. Planning for the four-car train began in 1944, and it made its public debut in spring 1947. It toured the United States and made high-profile visits to the Chicago Railroad Fair in 1948 and 1949. Afterward, the four-car set was sold to Union Pacific. *Solomon collection*

View of Illinois cornfields through tinted glass on the *Vista Dome* on Wabash's Chicago to St. Louis *Blue Bird* on July 21, 1958. Wabash's domeliner began operations on February 26, 1950, to entice passengers to the Wabash route. In addition to domes, the train featured specially commissioned murals by Auriel Bessemer illustrating historical and contemporary themes along the line. *Richard Jay Solomon*

continued from page 149

clearances, such as Boston & Albany. Each Astra Dome had elevated seats for 24 passengers. The whole train could carry up to 216 seated passengers.

The *Train of Tomorrow* showcased technologies from no less than five GM divisions. The air conditioning was the work of its Frigidaire Division. Its Styling Division focused on interior design, while its DELCO Division supplied generating units for each individual car. The locomotive was a specially decorated E7A built by GM's Electro-Motive Division.

General Motors wasted no time in putting its *Train of Tomorrow* in the public spotlight. On May 26 and 27, 1947, it operated a special roundtrip publicity extravaganza for journalists over the Monon between Chicago and French Lick, Indiana. (Ironically, Monon was among railroads that neither ordered dome cars nor E-units, although it was a customer for Electro-Motive F3s, which it used as both freight and passenger locomotives.) The trip was followed by meetings with industry executives and a weeklong public open house at Chicago, after which the train was sent on an aggressive 6-month, 30-city publicity tour. In 1948 and 1949, *Train of Tomorrow* was prominently displayed at the Chicago Railroad Fair. After its tour, the cars were sold to Union Pacific, which assigned it to a nameless service between Seattle and Portland, where it worked in relative obscurity for several years.

Bigger Domes

In the 1950s, the full-length dome with a greater seating capacity was developed, as an expansion of the popular *Astra/Vista Dome* concept.

First of the full-length designs was the *Superdome*, jointly developed by Milwaukee Road and Pullman in 1952. These were massive cars, among the heaviest ever built for an American railroad, and represent a complete departure from Milwaukee's 1930s lightweight philosophy. Pullman built ten Superdomes for service on the new Chicago–Seattle *Olympian Hiawatha* and Chicago–Milwaukee–Twin Cities *Hiawatha* trains. Each car had dome level seats for sixty-eight passengers—nearly three times the amount of *Vista Dome* cars used by other railways. The cars measured 85 feet long, 10 feet wide, and 15 feet 6 inches tall, and rode on six-wheel trucks. Significantly the domes carried their own built-in diesel-generator powerplant for heating and lighting independent of the rest of the train. Great Northern and Santa Fe also bought full-length domes for transcontinental service to augment their dome fleets.

In 1954, Southern Pacific introduced an unusual variation of the full-length dome for service on its *Daylight* trains. In addition to an elevated seating section where passengers could better take in the scenery, the dome extended 73 feet 4⅜ inches across a nonelevated open area featuring a bar that made for a cathedral ceilinglike effect quite unlike conventional railway passenger cars. Using components provided by Budd, SP built seven cars in two variations: one with a mix of coach and lounge seating on the elevated section, the other strictly lounge seating. California interior decorator Maurice Sands styled the passenger areas with "moss" green walls with Parkwood and rattan paneling, jade green upholstered seats, and light green lounge sofas. These domes were built without vestibules or side doors on the premise that they would always operate with other cars.

Historically, domes were rare on eastern lines. Baltimore & Ohio was an exception when they bought low-profile domes for Washington–Chicago service on its *New Columbian*, introduced in 1949. In an October 1949 advertisement B&O boasted, "The New Columbian . . . the only train in the East with a thrilling Strata-Dome car. It is a Diesel-Electric beauty—a glamour-liner from front to rear! At regular coach fares the *New Columbian* offers an exhilarating experience—passengers feel as if entering a new world."

BROOKS STEVENS

by John Gruber

When hiring Brooks Stevens to design its post–World War II trains, the Milwaukee Road turned to a hometown innovator for passenger cars to be built in its own Milwaukee Shops. Stevens' most spectacular achievement was the *Skytop Lounge*, the *Hiawatha*'s observation car; today one of these unique cars operates in the *Friends of the 261* steam train. It stood in front of the Milwaukee Art Museum in summer 2003 as a part of an exhibition, "Industrial Strength Design: How Brooks Stevens Shaped Your World."

Stevens (1911–1995), a Milwaukee-born industrial designer, brought a new perspective to styling. His designs include the Oscar Mayer Wienermobile, Miller beer bottles, and Harley Davidson motorcycles. A graduate of Cornell University, he founded Brooks Stevens Design Associates in 1933.

He started preparing initial design renderings for the *Olympian Hiawatha* in October 1945, according to information at the Brooks Stevens Archive at the Milwaukee Art Museum.

Stevens felt fortunate in that the Milwaukee Road was the only major railroad in the United States that plans and supervises the research and construction of new trains in its own car-building shops:

"We are confident that you will find the *Olympian* without peer in rail transportation. We believe we have accurately translated the desires and fancies of the American public into a friendly, homey, and comfortable vehicle of modern transport. However, what has been achieved is up to the public to decide," he stated.

In designer's notes, Stevens tells about the observation car. "Most striking innovation of the train's contour and make-up is the Skytop

Lounge which provides the aerodynamic stern for the 12-car train. This departure is a combination solar lounge and observation area with the dome enclosure 90 percent transparent. No measure of safety—either in car balance or strength—has been sacrificed to make this unique unit possible." Ten lounges were built, six by Pullman with sleeping rooms for the *Olympian Hiawatha*, and four for the *Twin Cities Hiawatha* with parlor car seating.

With the inauguration of the Seattle–Tacoma train on June 29, 1947 (minus the *Skytop Lounge*, which took longer to build), Stevens' attention turned to the *Twin Cities Hiawatha* and *Pioneer Limited*.

Summarizing his work on the Twin Cities trains in May 1948, Stevens said, "The general theme of the *Hiawatha* is bright, cheerful colors, a discrete use of woods and Formica in an effort to produce a homey interior in contrast to the regimented look of transportation equipment in general which may have had a very cold atmosphere, trimmed with chromium moldings and bizarre lighting schemes."

Stevens' accomplishments are chronicled in the *Milwaukee Journal Magazine*, Wisconsin (December 6, 1992). According to Paul G. Hayes, the writer, "Stevens' vision, salesmanship, and style helped define American life in the twentieth century."

Former Milwaukee Road Skytop lounge observation *Cedar Rapids* rolls toward Chicago Union Station on an excursion led by Milwaukee Road 4-8-4 steam locomotive 261 on June 22, 2004. Milwaukee's unique Skytop cars were designed by Brooks Stevens and built at the railroad's company shops in Milwaukee in the late 1940s. *Brian Solomon*

Amtrak's *Texas Chief* was pictured on September 9, 1971, at Chicago with one of Santa Fe's full-length Budd domes and three high-level cars (bought for the Chicago–Los Angeles *El Capitan*). On May 1, 1971, Amtrak had assumed operation of most American long-distance passenger trains, including Santa Fe's plush transcontinental runs. *George W. Kowanski*

Another low-level variation of the dome were three Pullman "Sun-roof lounge cars" built for Seaboard Air Line in 1956, which featured lounge areas illuminated with large panes of safety glass on the sides and ceiling.

In 1954, Santa Fe bought a pair of experimental high-level cars for service on its Chicago–Los Angeles *El Capitan*. An additional forty-seven cars were bought from Budd in 1956, and finally twenty-four more in 1964. These were 15 feet 6 inches tall, and 85 feet long. They were designed with passenger seating on the upper level with nonrevenue facilities such as crew dorms and dining areas on the lower levels. While bi-levels were common on many suburban services, especially in the Chicago area, Santa Fe's cars were rare examples of bi-level long distance passenger cars. They inspired Amtrak's *Superliners*, which have been standard equipment on many long-distance services since the early 1980s.

Streamliner Potpourri

In the decade following World War II, North American railroads introduced dozens of new streamlined trains that showcased new equipment and were aimed at encouraging continued passenger travel. The diesel-hauled streamlined limited was the new standard. In addition to re-equipping flagship trains streamlined before the war, a number of railroads that hadn't previously availed themselves of streamlining bought modern lightweight cars or diesels to introduce flashy new trains.

Yet, even after massive investment, streamliners represented a relatively small portion of railroad services. Ironically, it was in the 1960s, as railroads began hacking away at their long-distance schedules allowing for mass retirement of pre-streamlined heavyweight cars, that streamlined equipment finally attained a dominant role. By that time rail travel was in a downward spiral, and in 1971 Amtrak was formed to pick up the pieces.

All aboard the "PACEMAKER"

Setting the pace for the coach streamliners of tomorrow

Mealtime Money's Worth

Dinner or breakfast in the cheerful Pacemaker dining car is attractively served at an attractive price. And the scenic background of the Water Level Route furnishes a delightful setting.

First Date with Dad

This young lady's meeting her Navy Dad for the first time. So now she's beauty napping in the special Women's Coach, where the Maid watches over her while Mother's in the dining car.

Modern Slant on Sleep

At night, when coach lights are dimmed, the Pacemaker's individual pillow-soft seats can be slanted back to a sleep-inviting angle. Passengers who wish extra pillows can rent them for a trifle.

At the low cost of a coach ticket, this luxury train becomes yours from end to end. Rest in your own reserved, reclining chair. Freshen up in spacious, modern dressing rooms. Enjoy delightful, economical meals in the smart dining car. Or relax in a streamlined Observation Lounge.

NEW YORK CE[NTRAL]
THE WATER LEVEL RO[UTE]

New York Central System was America's second busiest passenger railroad. Its timetable lists numerous trains west from New York's Grand Central over its "Water Level Route" to midwestern hubs, including Chicago, St. Louis, Cincinnati, and Detroit. While its best-known train was the *20th Century Limited*, it operated a host of other streamlined limited trains, including the overnight New York–Chicago coach train called *The Pacemaker*. Solomon collection

Pennsylvania's *The Trail Blazer* was an overnight coach train equivalent to New York Central's *Pacemaker*. Both trains used modern lightweight streamlined cars in a service designed to appeal to budget travelers. *The Trail Blazer* was one of seven daily PRR express passenger trains between New York and Chicago. It departed New York Pennsylvania Station at 4:05 p.m. and arrived at Chicago Union Station at 7:55 a.m. the following morning. Solomon collection

RAILROADING IS *People*

Nothing in this world is as interesting as—people! Nothing is as important as people . . . people who live and grow, love and get married . . . people with their habits and manners, their likes and dislikes. Nothing really matters but—people.

The city? We think of it as people. The countryside is people. And so is the railroad . . . just folks — all of them!

THE TRAIL BLAZER

Locomotives, cars, equipment . . . all these have been thought out, designed, engineered, developed and built by people for people. They are of value only as they serve people.

We of the Pennsylvania Railroad try to keep in mind always: everything we do is measured by how we help people, how we get along with people, how we treat people. Our greatest reward is in having people think well of us . . . because we have served them well!

PENNSYLVANIA RAILROAD
Serving the Nation

BUY UNITED STATES VICTORY BONDS AND STAMPS

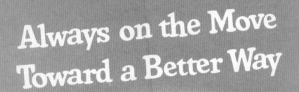

Always on the Move Toward a Better Way

Above: Santa Fe operated one of the best-known fleets of streamlined trains. These served the Southwest with style and class. It's famous slogan, "Santa Fe All the Way," covered trains such as *The Super Chief, The Chief, Texas Chief, San Francisco Chief, San Diegan, The Kansas Cityan, The Chicagoan, The Tulsan,* and *El Capitan. Solomon collection*

Above right: After World War II, most major American railroads introduced new streamlined trains. This Texas & Pacific ad from its 1947 public timetable reveals its plans to the riding public. By this time, streamlined trains conveyed luxury transport, smoother-riding cars with reclining seats, fluorescent lighting, and air-conditioning, all while running on expedited express schedules. There was no concern any longer for trivial operational issues such as aerodynamics. *Solomon collection*

Right: Texas Pacific Railway was part of the Missouri Pacific family and participated in operation of the *Texas Eagle* (trains 1 and 2) that connected El Paso, Texas, with St. Louis, Missouri. It carried through sleepers to Washington, DC, and New York City in conjunction with Pennsylvania Railroad. *Solomon collection*

After World War II, railroads across North America planned new streamlined trains. This November 1946 Missouri–Kansas–Texas (popularly known as the "Katy") advertisement anticipates the railroad's new *Texas Special* that would be jointly operated with St. Louis–San Francisco (known as the "Frisco") between St. Louis and Texas cities. The train made its debut in 1948 hauled by specially styled Electro-Motive E7s. *Solomon collection*

Scenery...Unlimited from B&O's STRATA-DOMES

Completely relaxed in a comfortable seat, you'll enjoy Nature's everchanging panorama of colorful scenery, from every angle as you glide along in B&O's thrilling Strata-Dome between Washington and Chicago. And there's no additional charge.

FLOODLIGHTS AT NIGHT
Powerful beams of light turn the landscape into a panorama of novel attractions!

Strata-Dome Dieseliners between

CHICAGO • AKRON
PITTSBURGH • WASHINGTON

The Capitol Limited
(All-Pullman with Stewardess-Nurse)

The Columbian
(Deluxe Coach with Stewardess-Nurse)

The Shenandoah*
(Pullman and Coach with Stewardess-Nurse)

Through service to and from Baltimore, Wilmington, Philadelphia and New York.

*On the Shenandoah, Strata-Dome is operated on alternate dates. Available only to Pullman passengers on the Shenandoah.

Strata-Domes are a B&O exclusiv

BALTIMORE & OHIO

NEW FEATURES on the CAPITOL LIMITED

LARGE, ULTRA-MODERN DINING CAR—B&O's fine food, moderately priced, courteously served in a relaxing atmosphere.

STEWARDESS SERVICE— The courteous, efficient B&O Stewardess-Nurse will be

Above: Baltimore & Ohio was among the few lines in the eastern United States to buy domes. *Solomon collection*

Right: Initially Pennsylvania Railroad's diesel passenger locomotive livery was stately dark Brunswick green with golden stripes, such as that introduced with the GG1 electrics in the mid-1930s. In the 1950s, PRR adopted a cherry shade of Tuscan red for some passenger locomotives such as this restored PRR E8A now operated by Philadelphia-based Juniata Terminal Company. *Brian Solomon*

One of the most unusual stories behind a streamlined electric locomotive was that of the so-called "Little Joes." Twenty of these massive, double-ended, streamlined motors were built during 1947–48 by General Electric for Soviet electrified railways when Cold War politics intervened, preventing delivery to their intended buyer. In the end, Milwaukee Road bought twelve, and were known as "Joes" after Soviet dictator Josef Stalin. Indiana interurban South Shore took three for its 1,500-volt DC lines, while the remainder were sold to the Paulista Railway in Brazil. Pictured on June 22, 1955, is an E76 working a freight near St. Regis, Montana, under 3,000-volt DC catenary. *John E. Pickett*

TOPS FOR TRAVEL TO AND FROM WASHINGTON

B & O's SILVER SPRING STATION
In Northwest Suburban Area

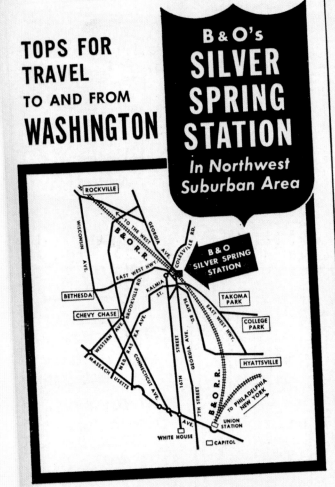

Enter and leave Washington the easy way . . . from B&O's complete and modern Silver Spring Station. All B&O through trains between the EAST and WEST stop here, saving you time and traffic worries.

There's plenty of free parking space, fast taxi service, and bus service *at the station*. You can also secure travel information, make reservations, and arrange for baggage handling.

The next time you plan a trip to Pittsburgh, Cleveland, Detroit, Chicago, Cincinnati, Louisville, St. Louis, Philadelphia, New York, the West or the Southwest—enjoy the convenience of B&O's Silver Spring Station!

Phone: JUniper 9-4343

ECONOMY – COMFORT
on B & O's DAYLIGHT SpeedLiners

(Trains 21 and 22) between

**PHILADELPHIA
WILMINGTON
BALTIMORE
WASHINGTON
CUMBERLAND
PITTSBURGH**

(connections at Pittsburgh to and from Youngstown and Cleveland)

You ride in modern, air-conditioned stainless steel coaches with soft reclining, reversible seats and wide picture windows. Smooth Diesel power . . . fast daylight schedules . . . in the diner—good food, moderately priced.

SAVE UP TO 1/3
on round-trip coach fares between

**PHILADELPHIA
BALTIMORE
WASHINGTON**
and
**MARTINSBURG
CUMBERLAND
PITTSBURGH**
and intermediate points

Return tickets good for 30 days. Children under 12, half-fare—under 5, free.

(Fares do not apply for local travel between Philadelphia and Washington and intermediate stations.)

Ask B&O Ticket Agent for details.

15

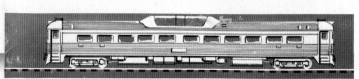

RDC

With the "New Look" *Budd*

CHAPTER 5

LIGHTWEIGHTS OF THE 1950s AND 1960s

The brief but intensive passenger rail resurgence during World War II only temporarily altered the overall decline in American passenger rail ridership. Despite the introduction of many glamorous new streamlined trains, by the early 1950s passenger traffic was again in a downward spiral. Railroads and equipment manufacturers again searched for innovative means to stem the declines. Recalling positive public response to the mid-1930s streamliners, plus a desire to cut operating costs, resulted in development of a new wave of trains that debuted in the mid-1950s.

The major passenger railcar manufacturers simultaneously refined new technologies for passenger train design, while General Motors developed its own innovative concept train, discussed in Chapter 4. Key to many of the new trains were streamlined, lightweight, low-center-of-gravity designs aimed at lowering construction costs and reducing operating

and maintenance expenses, while allowing for higher average speed, and in theory, greater passenger comfort.

It was hoped that reducing costs would translate into lower ticket prices and greater train frequency, which would help reverse passing traffic declines. A May 18, 1953, article on advance train design in *Railway Age* echoed this sentiment, noting, "Many observers are of the opinion that the greatest opportunity for reducing costs lie in the direction of lightweight, highly efficient train units."

Budd RDC

Among the first, and by far the most successful, innovative new passenger equipment was Budd Company's Rail Diesel Car or RDC. This was introduced in 1949, and although it featured a novel appearance, it was in effect an advanced revamping of the tried and true self-propelled railcar. Where the vast majority of the old gas-electric "doodlebugs" had used spark plug engines and electric transmissions, Budd's RDC was diesel powered with a hydraulic drive. While gas-electrics operated singly, RDCs were designed to operate in multiple, which made them more versatile. This gave railroads greater flexibility, since the cars could better serve variable traffic demands. The RDC's need not be relegated to light branch lines as were older self-propelled railcars, but could work any variety of passenger traffic.

The RDCs featured a decidedly modern appearance: they looked and felt like mini-streamliners, and like Budd's other trains, these were built using its patented shot-welded stainless steel. They looked good

---

Opposite top: Baltimore & Ohio called its Budd Rail Diesel Cars "Speedliners" and initially assigned them to long-distance services between Philadelphia, Baltimore, Washington, DC, and Pittsburgh. In later years it assigned RDCs to suburban services. *Solomon collection.*

Opposite bottom: Edward G. Budd, who early in his career worked on McKeen's motor cars, formed the company that decades later would return to the self-propelled railcar and enjoy considerable commercial success selling them to American railroads. The Budd Rail Diesel Car was one of the few successful postwar designs. *Solomon collection.*

Where Rock Island's TALGO features three-unit articulated rakes (pictured in the opposite photo), its General Motors *Aerotrains* consisted of sets of ten GMC bus bodies, such as those seen here at Englewood, Illinois. The bus bodies had distinctive parallelogram-shaped windows. *Richard Jay Solomon*

and were comfortable to ride. In many instances RDCs allowed railroads to simultaneously upgrade service while dramatically lowering operating costs.

New York Central was first to employ RDCs, introducing them on Boston & Albany local runs in 1950. The cars were known as "Beeliners," and New York Central dispatched attractive young women to hand out colorful brochures to prospective rail customers along the line. Budd's RDCs were largely sold to eastern railroads for suburban and medium-distance services, with Boston & Maine, New Haven, and New York Central being among the largest buyers. A few western lines sampled the cars as well, notably Western Pacific, which employed them for service as the *Zephyrette*. This was a long-distance service running more than 900 miles through the deserts and canyons between Salt Lake City and Oakland that complemented the *California Zephyr* Budd-built dome liner. Canadian railroads also made widespread use of the RDCs.

Not only were the "Budd cars," as the RDC's were popularly known, the most commercially successful of the innovative train designs, but by far they enjoyed the greatest longevity. Many cars served for decades, and a few remain in service as of 2014.

Low, Light, and Fast

Many of the advanced train designs tried various radical means of lowering costs including articulation, lightweight alloy construction, low-profile, low-center-of-gravity design, and widespread use of other modern materials. Related innovations included application of head-end power systems for heating and lighting in place of traditional steam heat, along with modern, more efficient interior lighting and air conditioning.

TALGO

In 1949, American Car & Foundry became involved with the Spanish TALGO project. ACF was contracted to build trains for the Spanish National Railways (known as *Red Nacional de los Ferrocarriles Españoles*, or RENFE) and a demonstrator train to show off to American railways. TALGO was a truly innovative train design invented by Spaniard Alejandro A. Goicoechea during the late 1930s and early 1940s. (The TALGO acronym combines the train's articulated design, the

name of its inventor and Goicoechea's partner, José Luis de Oriol y Urigüen, and so infers: Tren Articulado Ligero Goicoechea-Oriol.)

TALGO embodied many innovations that deviated from established railcar design. It used an exceptionally lightweight tubular body design and semi-permanently articulated car sets. Its most unusual feature was individual wheel pairs used in place of conventional swiveling "trucks." These were designed to minimize wheel wear while enabling a very low profile and low center of gravity car that was capable of high-speed operation through curves. The cars used low-alloy, high-tensile steel for framing, the superstructure was made of aircraft-grade aluminum, and the outer skin was composed of stainless steel. Its interior decor made intensive use of modern plastics, both to reduce weight and require less maintenance. Like other advanced trains, TALGO was a head-end power pioneer. An onboard auxiliary generator produced three-phase alternating current for train lighting and climate control.

In 1949 ACF demonstrated its experimental TALGO in the United States, notably running on the Lackawanna between Hoboken and Dover, New Jersey. However, there was little interest domestically, so it initially focused on its Spanish trains,

Rock Island was one of three classic American railroads to sample ACF's adaptation of the Spanish-designed lightweight TALGO train. Where the other TALGO operators, Boston & Maine and New Haven Railroads, opted for Fairbanks-Morse diesels in a push-pull arrangement, Rock Island bought one of Electro-Motive Division's LWT12 diesels to haul its train. Later, Rock Island picked up both General Motors *Aerotrain* sets, also powered by LWT12s, which has led to some confusion between the similar-looking trains. *John E. Pickett*

which involved several years of extensive testing and operation. Then in 1954, ACF's TALGO Project, under direction of J. Furrer, organized another demonstration tour for a specially designed train aimed at the American market, which could be hauled either by a standard locomotive or specially designed, modern lightweight diesels.

The ability to accelerate a light consist quickly and to operate much faster through curves were among the selling points. Furrer hoped to entice railroads with the prospect of being able to tighten schedules by up to 25 percent without dramatically raising top operating speeds, while lowering overall operating expenses.

Rock Island had been closely following the development of European lightweight trains and jumped on the opportunity to be the first railroad in the United

Boston & Maine's ACF TALGO train with Fairbanks-Morse light-weight locomotive model P12-42 was less than one year old when it was photographed near the Boston engine terminal on July 3, 1958. F-M built a total of four P12-42 diesel electric locomotives, two each for Boston & Maine and New Haven Railroad, to power ACF TALGO trains. In service, the New England TALGOs were poorly regarded and didn't last very long. *Richard J. Solomon*

States with a TALGO. *Railway Age* reported in June 1954 that Rock Island ordered a trainset to be hauled by a modern General Motors lightweight diesel. The price was $600,000 for an estimated public debut as its new Chicago–Peoria *Jet Rocket* in late 1955. As ordered, this was delivered with one of Electro-Motive Division's futuristic styled LWT12 diesels—the same model used to power GM's own lightweight *Aerotrain* (see opposite). In 1957 and 1958, Boston & Maine and New Haven both debuted ACF-built TALGO trains powered with streamlined Fairbanks-Morse "Speed Merchant" diesel locomotives at each end.

Train–X

Related to ACF's TALGO was Pullman-Standard's Train-X, which employed similar technology using articulated low-center-of-gravity bodies with guided single axles and advanced suspension. Robert R. Young was the primary patron of this novel train, encouraging

its development in 1947 when he was at the helm of Chesapeake & Ohio. Then, in the mid-1950s, after Young moved to New York Central, he ordered a five-car Train-X from Pullman for service as its *Xplorer*. Specially built low-profile Baldwin diesel-hydraulic locomotives using a modified "Shark nose" body style were ordered to power the train. New Haven ordered a similar train for service as the *Dan'l Webster*.

Aerotrain

General Motors *Aerotrain* was developed as a concept train aiming to achieve many of the same goals as TALGO and Train-X. Its chief engineer, B. B. Brownell, and GM's coordinator of new products, W. H. Harvey, detailed *Aerotrain* in December 26, 1955, *Railway Age*. The train took its name from its unique air-suspension system designed to work with single axles to provide a more comfortable ride. A network of eight air-bellows supported two axles on each car and used sophisticated pressure regulation to maintain carbodies at a constant level in regards to track structure.

Aerotrain's dynamic automotive styling shared qualities embodied by highway products of the mid-1950s, and yet its design was hoped to excite the public and distinguish the train as the latest concept in railway transport. GM hoped to reduce the train's production cost by adapting an established mass-produced

The cover of New York Central System's April 19, 1956, public timetable displays the railroad's latest lightweight streamliners for medium-distance service. General Motors *Aerotrain* operated experimentally on the Chicago–Detroit run, while the Pullman-built, Baldwin-powered *Xplorer* worked on the Big Four between Cleveland and Cincinnati. Both were unsuccessful. *Solomon collection.*

On January 13, 1956, New York Central displayed its borrowed General Motors *Aerotrain* at Albany, New York. This train was lettered for New York Central during its brief trial on its lines. *Jim Shaughnessy*

design, and so passenger cars were constructed from its nominally enlarged GMC 40 intercity bus bodies. These were 9 feet 6 inches wide, 10 feet 9 inches tall, and 40 feet long. Leading the train was the new Electro-Motive streamlined lightweight locomotive model LWT12, same as bought for Rock Island's TALGO. This was rated at half of a contemporary E9 passenger diesel powered by a 12-567C engine. Its exterior was finished in styled lightweight sheet steel. Among the innovative features of the locomotive was its head-end power system and dual auxiliary Detroit Diesel generator sets located in the locomotive nose.

General Motors built two *Aerotrains*, which made extended scheduled trial-service runs on Pennsylvania, New York Central, and Union Pacific railroads; the trains lettered respectively for their hosts. Following trials in Mexico, the trains were sold to Rock Island in 1958, which ultimately assigned them to Chicago suburban service along with its aforementioned TALGO that had been demoted from service on the Chicago–Peoria *Jet Rocket*.

Budd Tubular Train

Budd's low-floor, depressed-center Tubular train passenger cars were built in 1956 for Pennsylvania Railroad. The cars were 85 feet long, the same length as most modern standard-size passenger equipment, but were just 11 feet 9 inches tall, and weighed just 82,000 pounds, making them more than 30,000 pounds lighter than typical postwar streamlined cars. It was another head-end power pioneer. These were intended for intermediate-length travel and could be operated in conjunction with conventional equipment. Pennsylvania assigned its eight-car Tubular train cars to its twice-daily New York to Washington *Keystone* service, typically hauled by a GG1 electric, which towered over the train, making for an incongruous combination.

Low and Light, but Too Late

Despite innovative design and sophisticated suspension, *Aerotrain* and the other lightweights failed to emulate the success of the 1930s streamliners. They didn't meet the demands of daily transportation. Passengers found the lightly built, low-profile trains to be cramped, and they gave an uncomfortably rough ride. Within a few years of debut, most of the 1950s lightweight streamliners were withdrawn from

service, and the railroads struggled on with older conventional equipment.

Yet the trains were not all complete failures. Elements of Pullman's Train-X were incorporated in United Aircraft's TurboTrain of the mid-1960s.

Most successful has been advancements with the TALGO design. These were further refined and have enjoyed success in Spain and other European countries. In the United States, Amtrak took a renewed interest in TALGO's low-profile articulated pendular design in 1988. In the mid-1990s, it ordered several similar trains for service in the Pacific Northwest.

TurboTrains and *Metroliner*

In 1964, the debut of the sleek, fast, aerodynamic Japanese Shinkansen, colloquially known as the "bullet train," renewed an interest in advanced train development in the United States. The federal High Speed Ground Transportation Act of 1965 authorized funding for high-speed railway technology aimed largely at the Boston–New York–Washington "Northeast Corridor" (NEC) route.

In response, United Aircraft built a bi-directional, articulated, aerodynamic-streamlined passenger train powered by jet aircraft–style gas-turbines. UA had acquired Train-X technology that it further refined for TurboTrain's advanced suspension and guided axle system (aimed to minimize wheel-rail resistance when navigating curved track). The sophisticated pendular suspension was designed to minimize the effect of centrifugal forces on passengers when passing at high speed through curves. This enabled TurboTrain to take curves up to 46 percent faster than conventional equipment, which offered an attractive means of providing a faster, more comfortable service without the need for massive infrastructure improvement to existing lines.

TurboTrain's designers reverted to the original concept of streamlining by applying aerodynamic shapes perfected by wind-tunnel experiments. The

continued on page 170

Overleaf: On September 6, 1959, Pennsylvania Railroad GG1 4887 leads the afternoon *Keystone* under wire at Frankford Junction, Pennsylvania. The *Keystone* made two roundtrips daily between New York and Washington, DC. Budd's advanced Tubular train was unique to PRR and was retired after merger with New York Central in 1968. *Richard J. Solomon*

Budd's postwar exploration with low-profile design resulted in its "Tubular" train for Pennsylvania Railroad, which entered service in 1956. Among the advantages of Budd's train was that despite a lower profile, the cars could be operated with conventional equipment. PRR's Budd Tubular coach 9607 was photographed on August 17, 1958. *Richard J. Solomon*

Turboservice
BOSTON
PROVIDENCE
NEW HAVEN
NEW YORK

Effective June 26, 1970

	3001 DAILY	3005 Fri. only	3007 Sun. only	
	AM	AM	PM	
BOSTON ....Lv Back Bay Station	7:00	11:25	4:00	
ROUTE 128 .."	c7:10	c11:35	c4:10	
PROVIDENCE ."	7:39	12:04	4:39	
NEW LONDON "	8:31	12:56	5:31	
NEW HAVEN ."	9:20	1:45	6:20	
BRIDGEPORT ."	....	....	....	
NEW YORK ..Ar Grand Central Term.	10:39 AM	3:04 PM	7:39 PM	

	3002 DAILY	3004 Fri. only	3006 Sun. only	
	PM	PM	PM	
NEW YORK :.Lv Grand Central Term.	3:55	4:35	9:00	
BRIDGEPORT ."	c4:55	....	....	
NEW HAVEN ."	5:13	5:55	10:20	
NEW LONDON "	....	6:39	11:04	
PROVIDENCE ."	6:53	7:33	11:58	
ROUTE 128 ..Ar	d7:23	d8:03	d12:28	
BOSTON ....Ar Back Bay Station	7:34 PM	8:14 PM	12:39 AM	

c Stops only to receive passengers
d Stops only to discharge passengers

FORM 70   6-9-70   1st Ed.   ALLEN, LANE & SCOTT, PHILA.

Penn Central's June 1970 TurboTrain schedule. In less than a year's time, the service would be conveyed to Amtrak. *Solomon collection*

The cover of a brochure promoting United Aircraft's ultramodern TurboTrain depicts a model of a three-car set against a backdrop of the Boston skyline. The train was powered by five Pratt & Whitney 400-horsepower model ST-6B gas turbines and capable of tremendous speed. In service TurboTrain's top speeds were limited by restrictive infrastructure and the train never lived up to its potential. *Solomon collection*

United Aircraft's brochure boasted, "TurboTrain interior layout and décor resemble a jet airliner's interior. Carpeting and draperies, soft indirect lighting and individually controlled reading lights at each seat, fold-down tables, reclining seats with head rests, and carry-on luggage racks at the doors, are a few of the interior appointments contributing to passenger comfort." *Solomon collection*

continued from page 166
train shared common qualities with contemporary aircraft construction. It was constructed entirely from welded aluminum and weighed about half that of conventional diesel-hauled equipment.

UA contracted Pullman Standard to build its trains. In May 1967, TurboTrain made its public debut. To demonstrate its speed potential, in November 1967, dramatic public tests were conducted on a long tangent on Pennsylvania Railroad between New Brunswick and Trenton, New Jersey. In one exceptional run the test train reached an astounding 170.8

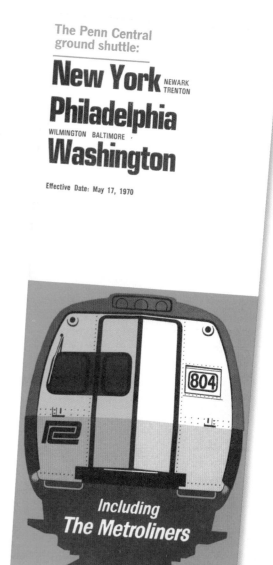

The Penn Central ground shuttle:

New York NEWARK TRENTON
Philadelphia
WILMINGTON BALTIMORE
Washington

Effective Date: May 17, 1970

Including The Metroliners

Congress passed the High Speed Ground Transportation Act in September 1965 that paved the way for both the Budd-built *Metroliner* electric multiple unit and United Aircraft's TurboTrain for high-speed Northeast Corridor service. The United Aircraft TurboTrain is seen testing on the Pennsylvania Railroad in February 1968. During one trial it hit a maximum speed of 171 miles per hour. *Richard Jay Solomon*

The Budd *Metroliner* was an advancement of its original 1930s-era lightweight designs and capable of great speed. However, with its flat front end, the electric speedster was hardly aerodynamic, and at best only notionally "streamlined." *Penn Central timetable, Solomon collection*

miles per hour. Scheduled services began in April 1969, when Penn Central put new TurboTrains on its Boston–Grand Central run. As with the 1930s demonstration trains, actual revenue service speeds were far less than the top speeds achieved in testing. In service, speed was limited to a conservative 100 miles per hour due to the condition of existing infrastructure on the former New Haven Railroad. Yet, the trains offered vast improvement to Boston–New York City schedules. Despite posted speed limits, some railroaders have suggested that the high-powered TurboTrain made a number of unofficial speed runs, well above the 100-miles-per-hour advised limit.

When Amtrak assumed operation of Penn-Central's long-distance services it inherited the UA TurboTrains. To increase capacity, Amtrak eventually expanded consists from three to five cars, and changed the New York terminus from Grand Central to Penn Station to allow passengers to make connections with its *Metroliner* high-speed electric services to Philadelphia, Baltimore, and Washington, DC. Canadian National also invested in TurboTrains, assigning them to the busy Montreal–Toronto corridor. While Amtrak's trains turned their last revenue miles in 1976, the Canadian trains survived in service under VIA Rail until 1982.

Amtrak inherited the United Aircraft TurboTrains. On February 12, 1976, a TurboTrain works as train 151 *Flying Yankee* at New Haven, on its way from Boston to New York City. It passes a former Pennsylvania Railroad GG1, which makes for a contrast between 1930s and 1960s streamlining. *George W. Kowanski*

Although the UA TurboTrains were relatively short-lived, in the early 1970s Amtrak invested in more bi-directional turbo trains of a streamlined French design. These operated for more than two decades before being replaced by locomotive-hauled trains.

The other noteworthy high-speed train development spurred by the 1965 High Speed Ground Transportation legislation was Pennsylvania Railroad's original *Metroliner*. Jointly developed by PRR and Budd, this super-fast lightweight electric train traced its roots back to Burlington's *Zephyr*. Budd built sixty-one shot-welded stainless-steel, self-propelled multiple-unit cars that featured a distinctive tubular design somewhat related to its 1950s Tubular Train previously described. Although lightweight and fast, *Metroliner*'s flat front was hardly aerodynamic.

The *Metroliner* project was begun by PRR, and the early cars featured PRR lettering and Keystones, but by the time the first *Metroliner* cars entered service in 1969, PRR had merged with New York Central forming

Penn-Central, and equipment was subsequently relettered with the PC logo. Like the TurboTrains, Amtrak inherited Penn-Central's *Metroliner* electric trains and the federal mandate to operate fast services. Amtrak later reverted to ordering electric locomotives and unpowered passenger cars for fast Northeast Corridor services, but the Budd stainless-steel multiple-unit cars served as the design basis for Amtrak's Budd-built "Amfleet" cars that became the backbone of its eastern services in the mid-1970s. Amtrak eventually assigned locomotive-hauled equipment to *Metroliner* fast services, and rebuilt many of the original cars for other work. Some of the old PRR *Metroliner* cabs survive to the present day in the form of push-pull, cab-control cars used in conjunction with a locomotive at the opposite end of the train.

Opposite top: In May 1970, a year before Amtrak assumed operation of intercity passenger services, a Penn Central TurboTrain is seen at Williamsbridge, The Bronx, New York. The TurboTrains were equipped with third-rail shoes to work in New York City electrified territory. *George W. Kowanski*

Opposite bottom: Penn Central's *Metroliner* approaches Newark, New Jersey, in April 1970. Amtrak's 1970s-era Budd-built "Amfleet" passenger cars were derived from the *Metroliner* cars and use a similar tubular welded stainless-steel design. *George W. Kowanski*

CHAPTER 6

PRESERVED STREAMLINERS

The innovative designs and shapely lightweight forms of the streamlined era continue to capture the American imagination. The classic trains built from the mid-1930s to the mid-1960s defined that era of railroading. Many of these great trains have been preserved, restored, and some continue to run, with a few classic streamliners remaining in daily service more than sixty years after they entered service.

Surviving streamlined trains represent a wide variety of the classic trains from a period roughly defined by the introduction of Union Pacific's M-10000 and Burlington's *Zephyr* in 1934, and continued through 1964 with production of the last Electro-Motive E9A. Electro-Motive's E- and F-units are the most common examples of streamlined locomotives, many of which have found their way into museum collections, tourist railroad service, remain active for use leading railroad executive office car specials, or toiling in relative obscurity on short lines. Furthermore, there remain hundreds of examples of classic lightweight passenger cars, many built by ACF, Budd, Pullman, and the St. Louis Car Company.

Opposite: In January 1938 Pennsylvania Railroad GG1 4859 was the first electric to arrive in Harrisburg, representing the last classic extension of the railroad's ambitious electrification. Five decades later in the summer of 1989, the old electric was proudly displayed on the platform wearing a recreation of its original Loewy-styled livery, complete with sans-serif Futura lettering and red trim around the cab windows. The 1937-built electric was installed under the Harrisburg shed in 1986. It is one of several GG1s on permanent display around the country. *Brian Solomon*

Many groundbreaking specimens are preserved for public display. Burlington's original *Zephyr* is at the Chicago Museum of Science and Industry, and Electro-Motive's FT freight diesel is at the St. Louis Museum of Transportation. However, you won't find any of the original 1930s Pullman/Electro-Motive articulated lightweight trains, nor Milwaukee Road's magnificent streamlined Atlantic or Hudson speedsters anywhere. These pioneering trainsets and engines, along with Pennsylvania's T1 and S1 *Duplexes*, were all scrapped. In fact, only a handful of American streamlined steam locomotives survive with their shrouding, notably Norfolk & Western's J-class No. 611—presently undergoing an operational restoration at the North Carolina Transportation Museum for its owner, Roanoke's Virginia Museum of Transportation. Other surviving examples of shrouded steam include Chesapeake & Ohio 4-6-4 490, displayed at the Baltimore & Ohio Railroad Museum at Mount Clare in Baltimore, and Southern Pacific's much-beloved 4449, dressed in its as-built *Daylight* scheme and shrouding, that makes periodic appearances hauling mainline excursions.

In the Spirit of Streamlining

Some museums have gone to great consideration to preserve historic equipment and maintain every element of "as-built" appearance and technology by working from period engineering documents, vintage photographs, and other materials. These machines display the precise look that streamliners conveyed when new. But not every example of surviving streamlined equipment has enjoyed the same degree of authentic preservation.

Electro-Motive's FT 103 goes for a spin on the turntable at North Carolina Transportation Museum's historic Spencer Shops during the "Streamliners at Spencer" event in May 2014. The FT was the first locomotive with a "bulldog nose"—the most common face of the streamlined era, which was applied to thousands of E- and F-unit locomotives. *Brian Solomon*

Not only have decades of intense service resulted in heavy wear, but necessary technological changes have often resulted in replacement of traditional machinery with more modern systems, as well as large-scale rebuilding that has often altered appearances.

By comparison, many tourist railways and other operators of streamlined equipment are more interested in maintaining the spirit of the streamlined era without concern for specific heritage or period details. Locomotives and cars are often operated in much-modified appearances that are deemed to best suit the goals of the organization. Locomotives may be dressed to represent similar equipment. Passenger cars from various origins may be painted for consistency to match a vintage trainset regardless of individual heritage. Some dinner trains and tourist train rides invent railway names and apply adapted paint schemes to vintage equipment. The popularity of the streamlined era has resulted in a variety of interpretive adaptations of period railway equipment including use as railway-themed restaurants and roadside attractions.

Iowa Pacific

Chicago-based Iowa Pacific Holdings is a private company involved in a variety of North American railroad ventures including the operation of tourist trains and re-created classic streamlined excursions. This includes its regularly scheduled high-end *Pullman Rail Journeys* experience between Chicago and New Orleans using restored classic streamlined cars attached to Amtrak's *City of New Orleans*. IP has been assembling an extensive fleet of vintage passenger cars and operates a variety of postwar streamlined equipment, most of it painted in a retro Illinois Central livery. Active cars include former Seaboard Air Line sleeper *Tallahassee*, now 9115 *Baton Rouge*; several former Great Northern

continued on page 183

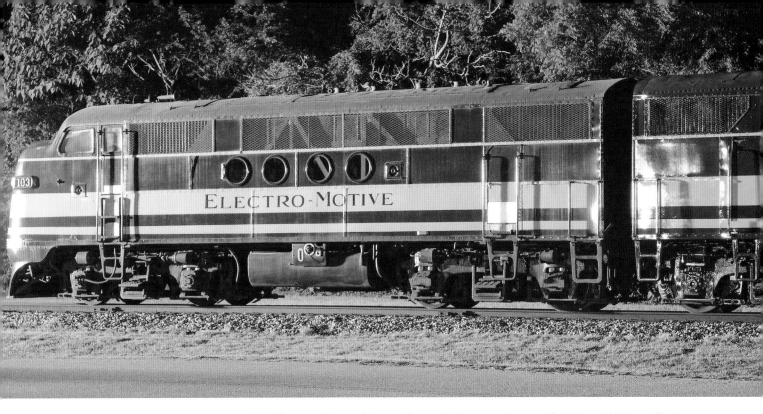

Electro-Motive's pioneer FT No. 103 was originally part of General Motors four-unit demonstration set. The FT model is immediately identifiable from later F-units by its row of four porthole windows. *Brian Solomon*

In April 1991, this fifty-year-old Pullman-Standard round-end observation rolled along at Black Butte, California, on the back of a re-created Southern Pacific *Daylight* consist led by Lima GS4 4449. Both the locomotive and observation car were built in 1941 for *Daylight* service. The vintage observation car is owned by the Northwest Rail Museum. *Brian Solomon*

Famous bulldog nose diesels from left to right: Union Pacific E9 949, Norfolk Southern executive F9 4271 (built as an F7A, upgraded by NS in 2006–2007), Erie E8A 833, New Haven dual-mode FL9 2019, Wabash F7A 1189 (built in London, Ontario), Chicago & North Western F7A 411. *Brian Solomon*

The great convergence of Electro-Motive's E- and F-units and Alco cab units at Spencer, North Carolina, in May and June 2014 displayed a variety of different models. Mixed in among the General Motors products are two examples of Alco-GE design: at far left is an Alco PA, built for Santa Fe but dressed as Nickel Plate Road 190, while tucked in at the far right is a Canadian National FPA4 built by Montreal Locomotive Works. *Brian Solomon*

Above: Electro-Motive's automotive-style mass-production often resulted in hundreds of diesels being built to nearly identical specifications with the paint scheme serving as the primary visual variation between locomotives on different railroads. Museums and historical groups can easily re-create locomotives long lost to scrappers by creative use of paint. Here, Delaware, Lackawanna & Western F3A 664 was originally built for Maine's Bangor & Aroostook but is cosmetically restored in this DL&W livery by present owner Anthracite Railroad Historical Society. For those who never saw a real DL&W F3A, it is the next best thing. *Brian Solomon*

Left: In a magnificent re-creation, Southern Pacific 4449 leads a streamlined *Daylight*-styled train across the curved viaduct at Redding, California. Appearance-wise, this train closely resembled one of SP's actual *Daylight* consists from the early 1940s, but the photo was exposed in September 1991. In its heyday, the *Daylight* was among the West's most recognizable passenger trains. *Brian Solomon*

continued from page 176
and Santa Fe full-length Budd domes; a former New York Central full-length diner, and former Florida East Coast sleeper *Caparra*, now car 9500 *Chebanse*. A pair of former Chicago & North Western E8s make convincing Illinois Central stand-ins on excursion runs.

Museums Preserve the Streamlined Era

All across North America are railroad museums dedicated to the preservation of equipment, artifacts, memorabilia, and photographs of the highlights of the railroad era. After the golden age of steam, the streamlined era remains one of the most popular periods for preservation and display.

Baltimore & Ohio Railroad Museum

Baltimore & Ohio Railroad Museum was one of America's first large efforts at railway preservation, and it houses many of the nation's most significant historic railroad equipment. This includes Baltimore & Ohio No. 51—the first Electro-Motive E-unit, two

Round-end observation No. 3310 *Pontchartrain Club* brings up the back of an Iowa Pacific Holdings excursion passing Libertyville, Illinois. In addition to special trains, Iowa Pacific regularly operates high-end Pullman Rail Journeys between Chicago and New Orleans using restored classic streamlined cars attached to Amtrak's *City of New Orleans*. *Chris Guss*

Opposite: The final four Alco PA diesels were former Santa Fe units operated by Delaware & Hudson into the mid-1970s. D&H sold these locomotives for service in Mexico in 1978. After decades without a PA in the United States, a pair of derelict former D&H units were repatriated thanks to the efforts of Doyle McCormack, who has since cosmetically re-created a unit that worked Nickel Plate Road. It was displayed at Spencer, North Carolina, in 2014. *Brian Solomon*

former Western Maryland diesels, F7A 236, typical of the vast number of postwar production F-units that characterized American dieselization, and BL2 81, an example of the relatively unusual semi-streamlined Electro-Motive model BL2 intended as a road-switcher

continued on page 187

Top: On October 5, 2014, a pair of Iowa Pacific E-units lead an excursion train at Fox Lake, Illinois. *Chris Guss*

Left: Iowa Pacific 9500 *Cabanse* was built in 1949 as a sleeping car for Florida East Coast, originally for service on the *Champion*. In the spirit of Illinois Central's named trains, these use cars painted like IC's postwar passenger fleet. *Chris Guss*

Above: Iowa Pacific's classically adorned pseudo-Illinois Central streamliner crosses Lake Monona at Madison, Wisconsin, on June 22, 2014, on a Wisconsin & Southern "rare mileage" trip. The third car in the passenger consist is full-length dome No. 551 *Sky View*, built by Budd as ATSF 551 in 1954. *John Gruber*

Opposite top: Two streamlined electric trains were built for high-speed *Electroliner* service on the Chicago, North Shore & Milwaukee in 1941. After North Shore ceased service in 1963, the trains were sent to Philadelphia where they worked as *Libertyliner*s on Red Arrow Line's former Philadelphia & Western line to Norristown (now SEPTA's route 100 suburban line). The trains were enormously popular with enthusiasts who dug deep into their pockets to save and preserve both trainsets. This one is cosmetically restored in its classic North Shore livery at the Illinois Railway Museum; the other is at the Rockhill Trolley Museum in Orbisonia, Pennsylvania. *Brian Solomon.*

Opposite bottom: *Electroliner* styling was the work of Chicago architect James F. Eppenstein, who provided the four-unit articulated trains with a modern design. There was nothing else like it on American rails. *Brian Solomon*

Right: The North Shore *Electroliner* is displayed at the Illinois Railway Museum. For twenty-two years this articulated speedster whisked passengers directly from the Chicago "L" Loop to the streets of downtown Milwaukee, Wisconsin. Service ended when North Shore was abandoned in January 1963. *Brian Solomon*

continued from page 183

type. Also on display is the above-mentioned C&O streamlined class L-1 4-6-4 490 that was styled for passenger service in 1946 and worked named trains including the *Sportsman* and the *George Washington.* In addition to locomotives, the museum displays several streamlined B&O passenger cars as well as one of its Budd RDC-2 railcars, known on B&O as a *Speedliner* and originally purchased for long-distance service before being reduced to working less glamorous commuter trains.

Railroad Museum of Pennsylvania

Among the finest railroad collections in the eastern states is located at the Railroad Museum of Pennsylvania in Strasburg. Like the B&O Museum, this boasts many unique artifacts and displays spanning all eras of American railroading, yet it focuses on Pennsylvania and its special role with railroading. As the home of the former Pennsylvania Railroad collection, this includes a wide variety of its steam locomotives, sadly none streamlined, but displays two GG1 electrics, including the 1934 prototype "Old Rivets," No. 4800, that is among the outdoor attractions to encourage visitors to peak inside. Other exhibits include Pennsylvania Railroad E7A 5901, the last of 428 E7As—once the most common of all streamlined

passenger diesels, and the model that essentially dieselized America's long-distance passenger trains after World War II. Philadelphia, Pennsylvania, was home to the Edward G. Budd Manufacturing Company, and there are several key examples of Budd stainless-steel production on display at Strasburg, including a round-end observation car built for Reading Company's 1937 *Crusader* that ran daily between Philadelphia and Jersey City, an RDC-1 that worked Lehigh Valley's Hazelton Branch, and an example of Pennsylvania Railroad's original high-speed *Metroliner* electric multiple unit.

Nine Lives of New Haven's FL9s

The final F-unit model was a unique design custom tailored for New Haven Railroad's unusual requirements necessary for operation to its two New York City passenger terminals. Built in two batches between 1956 and 1960, Electro-Motive's FL9 used a dual-mode

Baltimore & Ohio's EA No. 51 was the first Electro-Motive E-unit, the most common streamlined passenger locomotive in the early diesel era. It's preserved at the Baltimore & Ohio Railroad Museum in Baltimore, Maryland. Unfortunately, while the EA's streamlined body shell was preserved, its diesel engines and other internal equipment were removed before the locomotive was put on display. *Brian Solomon*

diesel-electric/electric arrangement to avoid creating asphyxiating pollution in the New York tunnels. In addition to working off the on-board diesel powerplant (typical of most North American diesel-electrics), the FL9 could also draw power from line-side third rail, as would a straight electric locomotive. The third-rail shoes were unusual in their own right as they could run on both the NYC's under-running electric rail and Penn Station's over-running rail.

The nonstandard configuration allowed the FL9 fleet to survive much longer than most conventional E- and F-style locomotives, and was among the last classic streamlined locomotives scheduled in daily passenger service. Today, several surviving FL9s have

been preserved to help maintain the memory of the New Haven.

The Railroad Museum of New England, based at Thomaston, Connecticut, is a nonprofit, volunteer organization closely affiliated with the Naugatuck Railroad. A majority of the equipment on the line represents southern New England heritage with a special emphasis on the New Haven Railroad. Among the locomotives at the museum are three former FL9s. Two were rebuilt in the 1980s by Chrome Crankshaft and repainted in the 1950s New Haven "McGinnis" livery. Locomotive 2019, original New Haven 2049, regularly operates on excursion trains. The third FL9 is the most significant, although it is awaiting restoration. Built in 1960, New Haven No. 2059 was the final one of 60 FL9s, making it the very last F-unit. It is also believed to be the most intact FL9.

Elsewhere in Connecticut; a pair of FL9s are displayed at the Danbury Railroad Museum, including one that had been painted in the New York Central lightning stripe livery by then owner Metro-North to commemorate 150 years of Hudson River rail service,

Above: After World War II, Chesapeake & Ohio rebuilt five class F-19 Pacifics into modern class L-1 Hudsons, Nos. 490 to 494, of which the first four received distinctive stainless-steel shrouds. Boiler jacket and front ends were painted in C&O's bright orange. The locomotives didn't survive long in service; however, engine 490, pictured in Cincinnati on August 10, 1947, was saved from scrapping and is now displayed at the B&O Museum in Baltimore. *J. R. Quinn collection, Solomon archive*

Left middle: Pennsylvania Railroad's GG1 prototype No. 4800, colloquially known as "Old Rivets," is among the outdoor displays at the Railroad Museum of Pennsylvania. *Brian Solomon*

Left bottom: The Railroad Museum of Pennsylvania at Strasburg displays the only surviving General Motors Electro-Motive Division E7A. Pennsylvania Railroad bought 46 E7As and 14 E7Bs between 1945 and 1949. Originally PRR's E7s were painted Brunswick green, although PRR 5901 is preserved in the mid-1950s Tuscan red livery with five gold pinstripes. *Brian Solomon*

Some old F-units have nine lives: Burlington Northern BN-1 was built in 1954 as Northern Pacific F9A No. 6700A, later it became BN No. 9800, then BN No. 766, before being converted into a rotary snowplow power pack. Then in 1989 and 1990, Burlington Northern reconverted this F9A and a B-unit back into locomotives to lead its executive passenger train. Today, now more than sixty years old, BN-1 is preserved at the Illinois Railway Museum at Union. *Brian Solomon*

while a lone FL9 has been preserved at the Eastern Connecticut Railroad Museum in Willimantic.

Maine Eastern maintains a pair of FL9s that were rebuilt and modified for Amtrak service by Morrison-Knudsen between 1978 and 1980 for service on its seasonal passenger service that runs between Rockland and Brunswick, Maine. This classy train emulates a 1950s streamliner using a small fleet of Budd-built stainless-steel cars, including former Pennsylvania Railroad observation/lounge *Alexander Hamilton* built in 1952.

Above: Today, Chicago, Burlington & Quincy *Zephyr* power unit 9908 *Silver Charger* looks pretty ancient. Curiously it was built by Electro-Motive in 1939 after introduction of its E-unit but designed to resemble the original 1934 *Zephyr.* It is preserved at the Museum of Transportation in St. Louis, Missouri, which also displays a variety of other significant equipment from the streamlined era. *Brian Solomon*

Right: Illinois Railway Museum has preserved the five-car 1936 Budd-built stainless-steel articulated Burlington *Nebraska Zephyr,* complete with round-end observation car *Juno,* and Burlington's Electro-Motive E5A diesel 9911A named *Silver Pilot.* *Brian Solomon*

Midwestern Museums

Located in the cornfields 60 miles west of Chicago near Union, Illinois, the Illinois Railway Museum has collected more than 375 pieces of railway equipment from across North America including: a Budd-built articulated *Nebraska Zephyr* set complete with the sole remaining Electro-Motive E5A diesel; one of two North Shore *Electroliner* interurban high-speed articulated trains built by St. Louis Car Company in 1941; Chicago & North Western F7A 411, built in 1949, and often operated with a 1950s-vintage

CN&W bi-level commuter train; and Union Pacific gas-turbine-electric No. 18, part of UP's 8,500-horsepower turbine fleet built in 1960. A variety of other Electro-Motive E- and F-units with regional significance, include locomotives restored for service in the 1990s as Burlington Northern executive units.

The Monticello Railway Museum in central Illinois displays and operates several restored classic diesels and streamlined lightweight cars including former Wabash F7A 1189, built by General Motors Diesel Limited in London, Ontario, for service on Wabash's Canadian

lines, and Canadian National FPA-4 6789 built in 1958 by Alco affiliate Montreal Locomotive Works.

Green Bay, Wisconsin, is home to the self-proclaimed National Railroad Museum, which displays a geographically diverse collection of streamlined equipment including: cosmetically restored Pennsylvania Railroad GG1 electric 4890; a General Motors *Aerotrain* complete with a LWT-12 locomotive and several of the lightweight four-wheel passenger cars made from GM bus bodies; Sir Nigel Gresley's highly refined class A4 Pacific *Dwight D. Eisenhower*, one of thirty-five steam engines built in Britain by London & North Eastern Railway between 1935 and 1938; and several F-units. (Years later the train was renamed in honor of the World War II general and later US president.)

Among the prized operating displays at the Lake Superior Railroad Museum in Duluth, Minnesota, is a finely restored former Soo Line FP7 No. 2500, a locomotive that was originally an Electro-Motive demonstrator. It is one of a few surviving examples of this passenger service F-unit model. This was 4 feet longer than a typical F7A to allow additional room in the car body for a large steam generator and water storage for passenger car steam heating—a technological carryover from the steam era. It also has one of the Erie Mining F9As, which were popular among railroad photographers for their continued operation in A-B-B-A set working heavy iron ore trains.

Above: The streamlined streetcar emerged in the mid-1930s with development of Presidents' Conference Committee Car. This technologically advanced trolley car featured the essential design of John W. Hession Jr. It was the most common type of modern streetcar with more than 5,000 built between 1936 and 1952. This Chicago PCC is preserved in working order at the Illinois Railway Museum. PCCs still work revenue services in several American cities including Boston, Philadelphia, and San Francisco. *Brian Solomon*

Opposite: Alco-GE designed and marketed diesels in the first decade of postwar dieselization. Among their most prominent models were FA/FB freight diesels and PA/PB passenger units. After Alco and GE parted ways in 1953, Alco's Canadian affiliate Montreal Locomotive Works continued to build FA-style locomotives for the domestic market. Among these were FPA4s such as Canadian National 6789, which has been preserved and restored by the Monticello Railway Museum in central Illinois. *Brian Solomon*

The St. Louis Museum of Transportation is home to one of the most significant collections of railroad equipment in North America, featuring several pioneering and/or technologically important pieces relevant to the streamlined era: Baltimore & Ohio No. 1, one of the nonstreamlined Electro-Motive Corporation boxcab diesels built in 1935 that served as a precursor to the E-unit of 1937; Electro-Motive pioneer FTA 103—the locomotive that sold dieselization to American railroads; Burlington's shovelnose power car *Silver Charger*, built in 1939, which resembles the

Southern Railway E8A 6900, dressed in the railroad's late-era passenger livery, is one of several operational E-units in the United States, exhibited here at the North Carolina Transportation Museum in Spencer, North Carolina. Compared with the large number of serviceable F-units, comparatively few E-units remain in working order. Their A1A trucks were designed for fast passenger service and lighter axle loads but make them much less useful for short lines and small tourist railroads. *Brian Solomon*

early *Zephyr* power cars constructed several years earlier; and Rock Island No. 3, a General Motors LW12 *Aerotrain* locomotive. It also has several lightweight passenger cars of which Missouri Pacific 750, a parlor-observation built by ACF in 1940, is the most unusual. This car has regional significance as it was a regular feature on the *Missouri River Eagle* for many years.

Streamliner Preservation in the South

Among places to experience classic streamlined equipment in the south is Roanoke's Virginia Museum of Transportation, which displayed N&W J-Class 611 for nearly twenty years before it was sent for operational restoration. Once the J has been returned to service it is certain to be one of America's premier railroad attractions.

The North Carolina Transportation Museum located at the former Southern Railway shops in Spencer displays several streamlined locomotives: Atlantic Coast Line E3A 501, Southern Railway E8A 6900 and FP7 6133. In May and June 2014, the North Carolina Transportation Museum hosted one of the greatest modern celebrations of the streamlined era called "Streamliners at Spencer," which involved orchestrated display of more than two dozen locomotives, most of them Electro-Motive E- and F-units, plus N&W 611 and an Alco PA diesel, as well as historic passenger cars and related equipment.

The Tennessee Central Railway Museum at Nashville maintains a significant collection of Budd-built lightweight cars—most of them built for Burlington and Santa Fe's postwar streamliners—for use on its popular excursion trains. A pair of former Bessemer & Lake Erie F7A diesels and a former New York Central E8A add to the aura of the streamlined era.

Norfolk & Western 611 is a rare example of a preserved streamlined steam locomotive. During the 1980s and 1990s it was restored to service and entertained tens of thousands of people working in excursion service on Norfolk Southern. Out of service since 1994, during 2014, No. 611 underwent a full restoration at North Carolina Transportation Museum's historic Spencer Shops. *Brian Solomon*

Above: In May and June 2014 North Carolina Transportation Museum at Spencer hosted a popular event that brought together more than two dozen historic locomotives: in addition to many Es and Fs, Norfolk & Western's streamlined J-Class 611 steam engine, and numerous vintage passenger cars were displayed.
Brian Solomon

Right: Night photography sessions at North Carolina Transportation Museum's "Streamliners at Spencer" event attracted hundreds of photographers aiming to re-create scenes of 1940s and 1950s railroading. Here a pseudo set of Delaware, Lackawanna & Western F3s poses with a freight.
Brian Solomon

California Dreams of Streamliners

In their heyday, the most famous transcontinental streamliners connected California with the heartland; Santa Fe's *Super Chief, Chief,* and *El Capitan,* Union Pacific's *City of Los Angeles,* the UP-Southern Pacific *City of San Francisco,* and the famed Burlington–Rio Grande–Western Pacific *California Zephyr.* In addition Southern Pacific's *Daylights* connected cities within California.

The California State Railroad Museum, one of the West's great railroad attractions, is suitably situated near the original terminus of the first Transcontinental Railroad in Old Sacramento, just a few blocks from the State Capitol. Here the streamlined era is well represented with an operable A-B pair of Santa Fe F-units dressed in Leland A. Knickerbocker's famous warbonnet livery; the last remaining Southern Pacific E9 that is dressed in the famous *Daylight* scheme; and former Western Pacific F7A 913, of the variety that once led the *California Zephyr* through the Feather River Canyon.

Among the locomotives and interpretive displays is the Santa Fe dining car *Cochiti,* built by Budd in 1937 for the original *Super Chief* streamliner. The car was retired in 1968 after three decades of transcontinental service but took a roundabout way to reach the museum, finally getting there in 1978. In the 1990s it was beautifully restored, and visitors may now walk through the car and absorb its classic art deco interior that plays on themes of the American Southwest. Santa Fe named its streamlined diners after well-known Native American Spanish pueblos, with *Cochiti* taking its name from Mission San Buenaventura de Cochiti located near the railroad's New Mexico namesake.

In contrast to the California State Railroad Museum's urban setting is the Western Pacific Railroad Museum located among the evergreens in the High Sierra alongside Union Pacific's former Western Pacific main line in Portola, California. This repository of classic railroad equipment focused on former WP pieces, including WP F-units and a collection of former Burlington and WP Budd-built passenger cars, allows for a faithful recreation of a mini-*California Zephyr.*

Executive Trains— Modern Domain of the Classic Streamliner

Streamliners were more than just passenger transportation. These trains put the railroads in a positive public spotlight and provided a modern sense of speed, style, and progress, demonstrating the ability

Southern Pacific's order for nine Electro-Motive E9A diesels in 1954 contained its final streamlined passenger diesels. After retirement, SP 6051 was preserved and restored in the colorful *Daylight* paint scheme by California State Railroad Museum at Sacramento. *Brian Solomon*

to move fast and efficiently. Even in their heyday, most streamliners never earned much money, but they were among the railroad's most effective advertising.

Today, all the major railroads, along with some of the smaller ones, maintain the tradition of the streamliner in various degrees with company executive trains. In recent years some railroads only operate the classic *continued on page 200*

Union Pacific's heritage fleet includes one of the largest active collections of postwar streamlined passenger cars in the United States. Dome coach *Columbine*, built by ACF in 1955, is among classic streamlined cars seen crossing Altamont Pass on the former Western Pacific in July 1992, when Union Pacific operated a series of excursions in the Bay Area of California in conjunction with a National Railroad Historical Society convention. *Brian Solomon*

Union Pacific's *Cheyenne* was built in 1956 by Pullman-Standard as a lounge car. A decade later UP rebuilt it as a business car with deluxe sleeping and dining accommodation for company officers. *Brian Solomon*

Pullman-Standard's round-end observation cars *Hickory Creek* and *Sandy Creek* were among the finest passenger cars on American rails. Constructed in 1948 for New York Central's first-class *20th Century Limited,* these luxurious cars featured extra-large rear windows to allow passengers to take the scenery of the lower Hudson Valley on their way from New York to Chicago. Both Pullmans survive and *Sandy Creek* is now owned by Norfolk Southern chief executive officer Wick Moorman and is often used as part of NS's office car train. *Brian Solomon*

continued from page 197

passenger cars, using generator cars for heating and lighting and opting to haul them with modern freight diesels. Others have gone all out and reacquired classic Es and Fs and specially outfitted them for office car service. For anyone lucky enough to see these trains trackside, the effect successfully captures the spirit of the streamliner. Today's business trains are just about as good as it gets.

In the mid-1990s, Kansas City Southern acquired classic passenger cars and four former VIA Rail Fs of Canadian National heritage for its executive train. Each of the four locomotives was symbolically renumbered and named for the location of KCS shops: KCS-1 *Meridian*, KCS-2 *Shreveport*, the F9B KCS-3 *Pittsburgh*, and KCS-4 *Vicksburg*. These were originally outshopped in glossy black with red-and-yellow trim that hinted at the classic livery used by its famed *Southern Belle* passenger train introduced in the late 1930s. In more recent years KCS readapted *Southern Belle*'s red,

orange, and black livery to its freight locomotives and likewise applied this retro-scheme to its executive train, which now looks very much like the classic passenger train.

Norfolk Southern is a relative latecomer to the retro-diesel powered executive train. During 2006–2007, under direction of new Chairman and Chief Executive Officer Charles "Wick" Moorman, Norfolk Southern acquired and rebuilt a group of classic F-units to form an A-B-B-A set to lead its classy business train. Moorman's personal private car, former New York Central *20th Century Limited* Pullman observation *Sandy Creek*, painted in Tuscan red to match the train, often brings up the rear of executive trips.

No other contemporary large railroad does a finer job of maintaining the spirit of heritage equipment than Union Pacific. UP, which helped pioneer the diesel streamliner, whose *City* streamliners were among the best known in the West, and which maintained its trains to high standards right up to their inclusion in Amtrak in 1971, has continued to field some of America's most authentic-looking vintage trains.

Although it conveyed most of its passenger equipment to Amtrak, UP retained a selection of streamlined equipment for excursion service and business trains. It also retained an operational passenger steam locomotive, Alco-built 4-8-4 No. 844, and Electro-Motive E9 951 built in 1955. This last E-unit was withdrawn from service in 1980 and was largely out of public view for many years. Then in

Kansas City Southern 1 leads a business train toward Chicago on Canadian Pacific's former Milwaukee Road line at Davis Junction, Illinois. This revised paint scheme emulates the look of KCS's premier *Southern Belle* streamliner. While *Southern Belle* was a daily scheduled passenger service running from Kansas City to New Orleans, the business train is only used for special occasions. *Chris Guss*

the 1990s, UP set out to re-create classic diesel-powered *City* streamliners, and reacquired its former E9A 949, which had been sold to Chicago & North Western in the early 1970s for Chicago suburban service (serving Chicago's Metro into the early 1990s), and former E9B 970B that had gone to Amtrak. These locomotives, along with its 951, were rebuilt, overhauled, and upgraded to modern standards by VMV at Paducah, Kentucky.

While its locomotives capture the most attention, UP's streamlined passenger car fleet separates it from most other classic train operations. Including business cars, this consists of more than forty cars, most of them postwar streamlined lightweights built by ACF, Pullman-Standard, and St. Louis Car Company.

Most are painted in its classic livery of Armour yellow and gray with red striping. One notable distinction between its heritage fleet and its traditional cars are the car names. Most have been renamed to commemorate Union Pacific history, and include the names of famous passenger trains operated by UP and its various component lines, such as ACF coaches *City of Salina*, *Katy Flyer*, and *Texas Eagle* (reflecting well-known services operated by UP, Katy, and Missouri Pacific, respectively). Others are named for important locations on the UP system, such as Pullman-Standard lounge *Cheyenne* built in 1956 and originally known as *Baker*, or famous and significant Union Pacific personalities and company officers, including the ACF dome lounge *Harriman* built in 1955.

ACKNOWLEDGMENTS

My interest in streamlined trains began with my early fascination with Pennsylvania Railroad's GG1 electrics and Electro-Motive's E- and F-units, locomotives that were still common when I was growing up. My father's O-gauge Lionel electric trains included a Pennsy GG1, some streamlined passenger cars, and later a set of Santa Fe's warbonnet-painted F3A diesels. A trip from Seattle to Minneapolis aboard Northern Pacific's Raymond Loewy–styled *North Coast Limited* introduced me to long-distance passenger travel, and most importantly, the thrill of riding in a Budd *Vista Dome*. My father and I made regular trips on the United Aircraft TurboTrain between Route 128 station and New York City, and streamlined PCC streetcars in Boston.

As a kid in the 1970s, I regularly perused a dog-eared copy of Pinkepank's original compendium of American diesels published as *The Diesel Spotter's Guide*. Here I found images of classic streamlined trains, including Union Pacific's wormlike Pullman-built speedsters and Burlington's stainless-steel *Zephyr*s. In school, I'd sketch these sleek machines on the back of my notebook pages, along with images of the GM *Aerotrain* and other streamlined trains from earlier generations. In 1984, I made my first trip to Chicago and made a special effort to visit Burlington's *Pioneer Zephyr* at the Museum of Science and Industry. Later quests for greater understanding came from reading Donald Bush's 1975 book *The Streamlined Decade*, Karl Zimmerman's 1977 title *The Remarkable GG1*, and books such as Al Staufer's *Pennsy Power* series.

Over the last twenty years, I've researched and written a variety of books on railroad locomotives, passenger trains, and railroad technology including those on EMD, Alco, and Baldwin locomotives, and Southern Pacific and Milwaukee Road passenger trains. During the course of this collective effort, I gradually pieced together a more complete understanding of streamlining, the development of diesel locomotives, the refinement of late era steam power, and the history of lightweight passenger trains. I've exposed and collected thousands of images. For this book, I've dug deeper, scouring the pages of mid-twentieth-century railway journals including *Railway Mechanical Engineer, Railway Age, Diesel Railway Traction*, reading through patents, railroad trade literature, and many of the books on American and overseas railroading. In addition to visiting dozen of American railway museums, I've visited Germany's Zeppelin Museum in Friedrichshafen, the Verkehrszentrum in Munich, and a preserved example of a high-speed streamlined diesel car at Leipzig.

Over the years, a great many people have helped me. My father not only introduced me to railroading, but lent his photographs, books, and vintage railroad timetables and brochures. He conveyed his experiences riding classic streamliners, and he helped me with proofreading. John Gruber, with whom I've coauthored several books, has helped in many ways, including writing profiles of key designers of streamlined trains and making introductions, while assisting with research. My late friend Bob Buck of Warren, Massachusetts, who guided my railroad interest in my early years, supplied many photographs and personal experiences. Thanks also to his sons Kenneth and Russell for their ongoing support. Kurt Bell and Nicholas Zmijewski assisted with my research at the Railroad Museum of Pennsylvania. California State Railroad Museum's Paul Hammond guided my photography at CSRM. Special thanks to Pat Yough for organizing trips, photography, and interviews. Howard Pincus and Hal Reiser at the Railroad Museum of New England answered many questions regarding the history, maintenance, and operation of FL9s and other locomotives. Tom Carver provided valuable Electro-Motive literature and organized for me a first-class F-unit experience on the Adirondack Scenic Railroad. The Irish Railway Record Society allowed me unrestricted access to their Dublin library. Over the years many photographers and railway experts have traveled with me and lent their expertise, driving skills, and perspective. Tim Doherty, Otto Vondrak, Doug Eisele, Kenneth Buck, Doug Moore, Doug Riddell, and Rich Reed are among those who supplied valuable research materials. Clark Johnson Jr. has provided train rides on vintage equipment and reminiscences of 1950s train travel.

Among the photographers and photo collectors who supplied images for consideration with this project are: Jim Shaughnessy, George C. Corey, Robert A. Buck, Patrick Yough, George W. Kowanski, Jay Williams, John E. Pickett, J. William Vigrass, Chris Guss, Steve Carlson, J. Michael Gruber, and my father, Richard Jay Solomon. John Gruber and Scott Lothes of the Center of Railroad Photography and Art assisted with photos from the Wallace W. Abbey collection.

Special thanks to Steve Casper, Dennis Pernu, and everyone at Voyageur Press who assisted for all their help from the conception of this title to its completion as a finished book. Without their hard work this book would not have been possible.

BIBLIOGRAPHY

Books

Alexander, Edwin P. *The Pennsylvania Railroad: A Pictorial History.* 1st ed. New York: W. W. Norton, 1947.

Allen, G. Freeman. *The Fastest Trains in the World.* London: Charles Scribner's Sons, 1978.

Anderson, Craig T. *Amtrak: The National Rail Passenger Corporation 1978–1979 Annual.* San Francisco: Rail Transportation Archives, 1978.

Archer, Robert F. *A History of the Lehigh Valley Railroad: Route of the Black Diamond.* Berkeley, CA: Howell-North Books, 1977.

Armstrong, John H. *The Railroad: What It Is, What It Does.* Omaha, NE: Simmons Boardman, 1982.

Beebe, Lucius. *The Central Pacific and the Southern Pacific Railroads.* Berkeley, CA: Howell-North Books, 1963.

Beebe, Lucius. *The Overland Limited.* Berkeley, CA: Howell-North Books, 1963.

Bezilla, Michael. *Electric Traction on the Pennsylvania Railroad 1895–1968.* State College, PA: Penn State Press, 1981.

Brown, John K. *The Baldwin Locomotive Works 1831–1915.* Baltimore: Johns Hopkins University Press, 1995.

Bruce, Alfred W. *The Steam Locomotive in America: Its Development in the Twentieth Century.* New York: Bonanza Books, 1952.

Bryant, Keith L. *History of the Atchison, Topeka and Santa Fe Railway.* New York: Macmillan, 1974.

Burgess, George, H., and Miles C. Kennedy, *Centennial History of the Pennsylvania Railroad.* Philadelphia: Pennsylvania Railroad Co., 1949.

Bush, Donald J. *The Streamlined Decade.* New York: George Braziller, 1975.

Churella, Albert J. *From Steam to Diesel.* Princeton, NJ: Princeton University Press, 1998

Conrad, J. David. *The Steam Locomotive Directory of North America.* Vols. I & II. Polo, IL: Transportation Trails, 1988.

Cook, Richard J. *Super Power Steam Locomotives.* San Marino, CA: Golden West Books, 1966.

Corliss, Carlton J., *Main Line of Mid-America: The Story of the Illinois Central.* New York: Creative Age Press, 1950.

Del Grosso, Robert C. *Burlington Northern 1980–1991 Annual.* Denver: Hyrail Productions, 1991.

DeNevi, Don. *The Western Pacific: Railroading Yesterday, Today and Tomorrow.* Seattle: Superior Publishing Co., 1978.

The Designs of Raymond Loewy. Washington, DC: Renwick Gallery/Smithsonian Institution Press, 1975.

Diesel Era. *The Revolutionary Diesel: EMC's FT.* Halifax, PA: Withers Publishing, 1994.

Dolzall, Gary W., and Stephen F. Dolzall. *Monon—The Hoosier Line.* Glendale, CA: Interurban Press, 1987.

Drury, George H. *Guide to North American Steam Locomotives.* Waukesha, WI: Kalmbach Publishing Co., 1993.

Dubin, Arthur D. *Some Classic Trains.* Milwaukee: Kalmbach Publishing Co., 1964.

———. *More Classic Trains.* Milwaukee: Kalmbach Publishing Co., 1974.

Duke, Donald. *Southern Pacific Steam Locomotives: A Pictorial Anthology of Western Railroading.* San Marino, CA: Golden West Books, 1962.

———. *Union Pacific in Southern California 1890–1990.* San Marino, CA: Golden West Books, 2005.

Duke, Donald, and Stan Kistler. *Santa Fe: Steel Rails through California.* San Marino, CA: Golden West Books, 1963.

Dunscomb, Guy L. *A Century of Southern Pacific Steam Locomotives.* Modesto, CA: Dunscomb, 1963.

Edison, William D., with H. L. Vail Jr. and C. M. Smith. *New York Central Diesel Locomotives.* Lynchburg, VA: TLC Publishing, 1995.

Encyclopedia of American Business History and Biography: Railroads in the Nineteenth Century. New York: Bruccoli Clark Layman, Inc., and Facts on File, Inc., 1988.

Farrington, S. Kip, Jr. *Railroading from the Head End.* New York: Doubleday, Doran & Co., 1943.

———. *Railroads at War.* New York: Samuel Curl, 1944.

———. *Railroading from the Rear End.* New York: Coward-McCann, Inc., 1946.

———. *Railroading the Modern Way.* New York: Coward-McCann, Inc., 1951.

Garmany, John B. *Southern Pacific Dieselization.* Edmonds, WA: Pacific Fast Mail, 1985.

Greenberg, William T. Jr., and Frederick A. Kramer with Theodore F. Gleichmann Jr. *The Handsomest Trains in the World: Passenger Service on the Lehigh Valley Railroad.* Westfield, NJ: Bells & Whistles, 1978.

Gruber, John, and Brian Solomon. *The Milwaukee Road's Hiawathas.* St. Paul, MN: MBI, 2006.

Harlow, Alvin F. *The Road of the Century.* New York: Creative Age Press, 1947.

Hayes, William Edward. *Iron Road to Empire: The History of the Rock Island Lines.* Wolfe Book Co., 1953.

Henry, Robert S. *On the Railroad.* New York: Saalfield Publishing Co., 1936.

Hidy, Ralph W., Muriel E. Hidy, and Roy V. Scott, with Don L. Hofsommer. *The Great Northern Railway.* Boston: Harvard Business School Press, 1988.

Hollingsworth, Brian. *Modern Trains.* London: 1985.

Hollingsworth, Brian, and Arthur Cook. *Modern Locomotives.* London: Greenwich Editions, 1983.

Interurban to Milwaukee—Bulletin 103. Chicago: Central Electric Railfans' Association, 1962.

Jodard, Paul. *Raymond Loewy.* London: Taplinger Publishing Company, 1992.

Johnston, Bob, with Joe Walsh and Mike Schafer. *The Art of the Streamliner*. New York: Metro Books, 2001.

Keilty, Edmund. *Interurbans Without Wires: The Rail Motorcar in the United States*. Glendale, CA: Interurbans, 1979.

Kiefer, P. W. *A Practical Evaluation of Railroad Motive Power*. New York: Steam Locomotive Research Institute, 1948.

Kirkland, John F. *Dawn of the Diesel Age*. Pasadena, CA: Interurban Press, 1994.

———. *The Diesel Builders Vols. I, II, and III*. Glendale, CA: Interurban Press, 1983.

Klein, Maury. *Union Pacific, Vols. I & II*. New York: Doubleday, 1989.

Kratville, William, and Harold E. Ranks. *Motive Power of the Union Pacific*. Omaha, NE: Barnhart Press, 1958.

Liljestrand, Robert A., and David R. Sweetland. *Equipment of the Boston & Maine Vol. I*. n.d., n.p.

Loewy, Raymond. *The Locomotive (Its Esthetics)*. New York: n.p., 1937.

Marre, Louis A. *Diesel Locomotives: The First 50 Years*. Waukesha, WI: Kalmbach Publishing Company, 1995.

Marre, Louis A., and Jerry A. Pinkepank. *The Contemporary Diesel Spotter's Guide*. Milwaukee: Kalmbach Publishing, 1985.

McDonald, Charles W. *Diesel Locomotive Rosters*. Milwaukee: Kalmbach Publishing, 1982

Middleton, William D. *When the Steam Railroads Electrified*. Milwaukee: Kalmbach Publishing, 1974.

Mulhearn, Daniel J., and John R. Taibi. *General Motors' F-Units: The Locomotives that Revolutionized Railroading*. New York: Quadrant Press, Inc., 1982.

Overton, Richard, C. *Burlington West*. Cambridge, MA: Harvard University Press, 1941.

———. *Burlington Route: A History of the Burlington Lines*. New York: Alfred A. Knopf, 1965.

Pinkepank, Jerry A. *The Diesel Spotter's Guide*. Milwaukee: Kalmbach Publishing, 1967.

———. *The Second Diesel Spotter's Guide*. Milwaukee: Kalmbach Publishing, 1973.

Pope, Dan, and Mark Lynn. *Warbonnets: From Super Chief to Super Fleet*. Waukesha, WI: Pentrex, Inc., 1994.

Ransome-Wallis, P. *World Railway Locomotives*. New York: Hawthorn Books, 1959.

Reck, Franklin M. *On Time*. Electro-Motive Division of General Motors, 1948.

———. *The Dilworth Story*. New York: Nabu Press, 1954.

Rose, Joseph R. *American Wartime Transportation*. New York: American Economic Association, 1953.

Ryan, Dennis, and Joseph Shine. *Southern Pacific Passenger Trains Vols. 1 & 2*. La Mirada, CA: Four Ways West Publications, 1986, 2000.

Saunders, Richard, Jr. *The Railroad Mergers and the Coming of Conrail*. Westport, CT: Greenwood, 1978.

———. *Merging Lines: American Railroads 1900–1970*. DeKalb, IL: Northern Illinois University Press ,2001.

Schafer, Mike, with Joe Walsh. *Classic American Streamliners*. Osceola, WI: MBI, 1997.

Schafer, Mike, and Brian Solomon. *Pennsylvania Railroad*. Minneapolis: Voyageur Press, 2009.

Schrenk, Lorenz P., and Robert L. Frey. *Northern Pacific Diesel Era 1945–1970*. San Marino, CA: Golden West Books, 1988.

Signor, John R. *Tehachapi*. San Marino, CA: Golden West Books, 1983.

———. *Donner Pass: Southern Pacific's Sierra Crossing*. San Marino, CA: Golden West Books, 1985.

Solomon, Brian. *The American Steam Locomotive*. Osceola, WI: MBI, 1998.

———. *Southern Pacific Railroad*. Osceola, WI: MBI, 1999.

———. *The American Diesel Locomotive*. Osceola, WI: MBI, 2000.

———. *Locomotive*. Osceola, WI: MBI, 2001.

———. *Railway Masterpieces: Celebrating the World's Greatest Trains, Stations and Feats of Engineering*. Iola, WI: Krause, 2002.

———. *Amtrak*. St. Paul, MN: MBI, 2004.

———. *Burlington Northern Santa Fe Railway*. St. Paul, MN: MBI, 2005.

———. *CSX*. St. Paul, MN: MBI, 2005.

———. *EMD F-unit Locomotives*. North Branch, MN: Specialty Press, 2005.

———. *Southern Pacific Passenger Trains*. St. Paul, MN: MBI, 2005.

———. *EMD Locomotives*. St. Paul, MN: MBI, 2006.

———. *Alco Locomotives*. St. Paul, MN: MBI 2009.

———. *Electro-Motive E-Units and F-Units*. St. Paul, MN: MBI, 2011.

Solomon, Brian, and Mike Schafer. *New York Central Railroad*. Osceola, WI: MBI, 1999.

Stegmaier, Harry. *Southern Pacific Passenger Train Consists and Cars 1955–58*. Lynchburg, VA: TLC Publishing, 2001.

Strapac, Joseph A. *Southern Pacific Review 1952–82*. Huntington Beach, CA: Shade Tree Books, 1983.

———. *Southern Pacific Review 1953–1985*. Huntington Beach, CA: Shade Tree Books, 1986

———. *Southern Pacific Historic Diesels, Vols. 3–10*. Huntington Beach, CA, and Bellflower, CA: Shade Tree Books, 2003.

———. *Southern Pacific Motive Power Annuals 1967–1968, 1970, 1971, 1972*. Burlingame, CA: 1968–1972.

Staufer, Alvin F. *C&O Power: Steam and Diesel Locomotives of the Chesapeake and Ohio Railway, 1900–1965*. Carrollton, OH: A. F. Staufer, 1965.

———. *Pennsy Power II*. Medina, OH: A. F. Staufer, 1968.

Staufer, Alvin F., and Edward L. May. *New York Central's Later Power 1910–1968*. Medina, OH: A. F. Staufer, 1981.

Steinbrenner, Richard T. *The American Locomotive Company: A Centennial Remembrance*. Warren, NJ: On Track Publishers, LLC, 2003.

Thompson, Gregory Lee. *The Passenger Train in the Motor Age: California's Rail and Bus Industries, 1910–1941 (Historical Perspectives on Business Enterprise)*. Columbus: Ohio State University Press, 1993.

Waters, L. L. *Steel Trails to Santa Fe*. Lawrence, KS: Literary Licensing, LLC, 1950.

Westing, Frederick. *The Locomotives that Baldwin Built*. Seattle: Bonanza Books, 1966.

———. *Erie Power: Steam and Diesel Locomotives of the Erie Railroad from 1840 to 1970*. Medina, OH: A. F. Staufer, 1970.

White, John H., Jr., *A History of the American Locomotive—Its Development: 1830–1880*. Baltimore: Johns Hopkins University Press, 1968.

———. *The American Railroad Passenger Car, Vols. I & II*. Baltimore: Johns Hopkins University Press, 1978.

Wright, Richard K. *Southern Pacific Daylight*. Thousand Oaks, CA: RKW Publications, 1970.

———. *America's Bicentennial Queen Engine 4449*. Oakhurst, CA: privately published, 1975.

Zimmermann, Karl R. *The Remarkable GG1*. New York: Quadrant Press, 1977.

Periodicals

Classic Trains. Waukesha, WI.

Diesel Era. Halifax, PA.

Diesel Railway Traction, supplement to *Railway Gazette* (UK). (merged into *Railway Gazette*).

Extra 2200 South, Cincinnati, OH.

Jane's World Railways. London.

Locomotive & Railway Preservation. Waukesha, WI. [no longer published]

Official Guide to the Railways. New York.

RailNews. Waukesha, WI. [no longer published]

Railroad History, formerly *Railway and Locomotive Historical Society Bulletin*. Boston, MA.

Railway Age. Chicago and New York.

Railway Mechanical Engineer. Chicago and New York.

Railway Signaling and Communications, formerly *The Railway Signal Engineer* nee, *Railway*

San Francisco Chronicle. San Francisco.

San Francisco Examiner. San Francisco.

Signaling. Chicago and New York.

Shoreliner. Grafton, MA.

Southern Pacific Bulletin. San Francisco.

The Railway Gazette, London.

Today's Railways, Sheffield, UK.

Trains. Waukesha, WI.

Vintage Rails. Waukesha, WI. [no longer published]

Manuals, Timetables, Brochures

Amtrak public timetables, 1971 to 2008.

Baldwin Locomotive Works. Operator's Manual. No. DS-100. *Diesel-Electric Passenger Locomotive*. Philadelphia, 1947.

Baldwin Locomotive Works. *6,000 H.P Diesel Electric Road Freight Locomotives*. Philadelphia, 1949.

Central of Georgia public timetable 1959–60.

Chicago, Burlington & Quincy. *Burlington's big new Vista-Dome Denver Zephyr*. Chicago, Milwaukee, St. Paul & Pacific public timetables 1943–1966.

Chicago & North Western System public timetables 1945–1960.

General Motors. *Electro-Motive Division Operating Passenger Locomotive Manual No. 2300*. La Grange, IL, 1945.

General Motors. *Electro-Motive Division Model F3 Operating Manual No. 2308B*. La Grange, IL, 1948.

General Motors. *Electro-Motive Division Model F7 Operating Manual No. 2310*. La Grange, IL, 1951.

General Motors. *Electro-Motive Division Model F9 Operating Manual No. 2315*. La Grange, IL, 1954.

New York Central System public timetables 1943–1968.

Pennsylvania Railroad public timetables 1942–1968.

Pennsylvania Railroad. *Modern Power for Today's Trains*. No date.

Reading Company public timetable 1946.

Santa Fe public timetables 1943–1969.

Southern Pacific Company, public timetables 1930 to 1958.

Southern Pacific. *Your Daylight Trip*, 1939.

Southern Pacific. *Your Daylight Trip, Morning Daylight*, 1949.

Steamtown National Historic Site. *The Nation's Living Railroad Museum*. No Date.

Texas and Pacific public timetable 1959.

TurboTrain™ *Rail Speed, Convenience, Comfort*. United Aircraft Corporate System Center. Circa 1967.

United States Patents

49,227. Aug. 8, 1965. S. R. Calthrop.

489,911. Jan 17, 1893. F. U. Adams.

490,057. Jan 17, 1893. F. U. Adams.

809,974. Jan 16, 1906. W. R. McKeen Jr.

809,974. Jan 16, 1906. W. R. McKeen Jr.

972,467. October 11, 1910. W. R. McKeen Jr.

972,502. October 25, 1910. E.H. Harriman and W. R. McKeen Jr.

973,622. October 25, 1910. E. G. Budd.

1,628,595. May 10, 1927. F. Kruckenberg, et al.

1,631,269. June 7, 1927. P. Jaray.

1,727,070. Sept. 3, 1929. F. Kruckenberg, et al.

1,927,072. Sept. 19, 1933. E. J. W. Ragsdale.

2,079,748. May 11, 1937. Martin Blomberg.

2,093,579. Sept. 21, 1937. W. B. Stout.

2,095,883. Oct. 12, 1937, W. C. Meyer.

2,128,490. Aug. 30, 1938. R. G. F. Loewy, et al.

2,129,235. Sept. 6, 1938. E. J. W. Ragsdale, et al.

2,143,547. Jan 10, 1939. A. G. Dean.

2,171,425. Aug 29, 1939. A. G. Dean.

2,243,808. May 27, 1941. E. J. W. Ragsdale, et al.

2,247,273. June 24, 1941. Martin Blomberg.

2,252,209. Nov. 9, 1939. J. W. Patton.

2,256,493. Sept 23, 1941. E. J. W. Ragsdale, et al.

2,256,494. Sept 23, 1941. E. J. W. Ragsdale, et al.

2,575,454. Nov. 20, 1951. O. A. Kuhler.

2,595,858. May 6, 1952. O. A. Kuhler.

United States Design Patents

Des. 38,860. Oct. 15, 1907. W. R. McKeen Jr.

Des. 92,511. June 19, 1934. N. Bel Geddes.

Des. 93,809. Nov. 13, 1934. N. Bel Geddes.

Des. 98,133. Jan. 7, 1936. E. J. W. Ragsdale.

Des. 102, 600. Dec. 29, 1936. E. J. W. Ragsdale.

Des. 105,533. Aug 3, 1937. R. G. F. Loewy.

Des. 105,993. Sept. 7, 1937. R. G. F. Loewy.

Des. 106,143. Sept. 21, 1937. R. G. F. Loewy.

Des. 106,907. Nov. 9, 1937 I. C. Barlow, et al.

Des. 106,918. Nov. 9, 1937. H. L. Hamilton, et al.

Des. 106,920. Nov. 9, 1937. H. L. Hamilton, et al.

Des. 109,538. May 3, 1938. C. B. Stevens

Des. 113,009. Jan. 24, 1939. R. Loewy.

Des. 113,563. Feb. 28, 1939. L. A. Knickerbocker.

Des. 121,219. June 25, 1940. O. Kuhler.

Des. 136,259. Aug. 31, 1943. R. G. F. Loewy.

Des. 136,260. Aug. 31, 1943. R. G. F. Loewy.

Des. 146,545. April 1, 1947. O. Kuhler.

Des. 164,921. Oct 23, 1951. A. B. Girardy et al.

INDEX

ABOUT THE AUTHOR

Brian Solomon has authored more than fifty books on railroads, including *North American Railroad Family Trees*, *North American Railroads*, *Coal Trains*, *Railroads of California*, *Railroads of Pennsylvania*, *North American Railroad Bridges*, *Amtrak*, and *Railroad Signaling*. He is currently producing a popular railway photography blog called *Tracking the Light* (www.briansolomon.com/trackingthelight/) and divides his time between the United States and Europe to photograph and research railway operations. His photography has also appeared in the pages of many rail magazines, including *Trains* magazine, *Railway Age*, *Railroad Explorer*, Germany's *Modelleisenbahner*, and the *Journal of the Irish Railway Record Society*.